WINGS OVER WATER

Other Books by Walt Franklin:

Streamwalker's Journey: Fishing the Triple Divide
Wood Thrush Books
(personal essays)

Beautiful Like a Mayfly
Wood Thrush Books
(personal essays)

River's Edge: A Fly-Fishing Realm
Wood Thrush Books
(personal essays)

A Rivertop Journal
Writers Publishing Cooperative
(personal essays)

Sand & Sage: The Trails Beyond
Great Elm Press
(personal essays)

The Singing Groves
Timberline Press
(essay)

Earthstars, Chanterelles, Destroying Angels
FootHills Publishing
poetry

Uplands Haunted by the Sea
Great Elm Press
(poetry)

The Wild Trout
Nightshade Press
(poetry)

WINGS OVER WATER

The Late Notes of a Naturalist

by

Walt Franklin

Wood Thrush Books

Published by: Wood Thrush Books
                  27 Maple Grove Estates
                  Swanton, Vermont 05488

ISBN 978-1-7345175-0-7

Acknowledgements

Special thanks go out to the following individuals whose help assisted the production of this work in one capacity or another: Scott Cornett, Tim Didas, Brent Franklin, Leighanne Franklin, Dr. Allen Kerkeslager, Howard Levett, Pete McKenna, Walt McLaughlin, Daniel Redmond, Dr. Pete Ryan, Bob Stanton, and Jesse Vaughn.

The author also wishes to thank the many readers and supporters of *Rivertop Rambles*, his blog at **www.rivertoprambles.wordpress.com**, who helped inspire numerous outings in a quest for peace and understanding of the natural world in which we live.

Table Of Contents

Preface

This book begins and ends with visions from Dryden Hill, my outlook from the rural acreage where I've lived for many years. I had wanted to write a volume that included my passion for fly-fishing and the natural world, but didn't want its content to repeat, or strictly echo, the material of my previous books. *Wings Over Water* needed to be more than that; it needed to be different.

A river runs through the essays linked together in this work, but it's not the river made famous in Norman Maclean's wondrous novel. My river does have twists and turns, however, in familiar country. As an angler loving Nature in its widest and wildest manifestations, I've tried to write of this river and its personalities in both the metaphorical and the literal sense. I suspect that it's a river flowing at some level through the heart of everyone. It calls out occasionally for our attention. As an amateur naturalist, I've tried to reflect the river's various temperaments in a manner that invites the reader to approach and walk along in comfort.

The 14 essays in this book, bound by dreams and first-hand experience, are filled with people, things and places. You'll encounter streams and lakes and rivers, trout and birds and columbines, western travel and eastern home life. You'll discover art and poetry and science, myth and natural history, humor and sobriety, resistance and embracement. That may sound like a wild and crazy mixture, but I'm betting you will have an easy and informative journey—like a heron's flight along a winding stream. These essays may resist categorization or a simple fit between the banks of traditional genre, but I'm hoping they speak with the clarity of sparkling air and flowing water.

I was told once that my writing style seems to alternate intentionally between a detailed architectural prose and a form of gentle poetry. I think that's a fair assessment, although the alternation may be less intentional than it is impulsive. A reviewer of my book, *River's Edge* (2008), spoke kindly with some words I'd like to share now, since they also lay the groundwork of this very different *Wings Over Water*. The reviewer said, "It's not the technical aspects of fly-fishing that interests me. It's the discovery of nature and the creatures that share my outing that satisfies... I told my wife to read this... I said, all my other books on fly-fishing tell me *how* to fish. This book tells me *why*."

– Walt Franklin

WINGS OVER WATER

Views from Dryden Hill

1

I walked from the hollow underneath a leaden sky. In a bare-bones season all I carried for the hike was a camera, binoculars and walking stick. I passed through my grove of evergreens, knowing it was almost time for the annual "thinning of pines" ritual. At the end of each year I take a handsaw and remove dead branches plus a smattering of invasive spruce. For me, pruning isn't a vain attempt to manage nature or to bring order out of chaos. Rather, it's a vain attempt to have some fun while struggling to get a handle on the Norway spruce "invasion" and to clarify my vision. I like to think that my annual labor helps the new year's sun begin its penetration into the dense grove.

So, what was *this*? A sculpted evergreen the size of a bowling ball, its twigs, moss, leaves and grasses interwoven to a sphere and lying on the ground beneath the spruce trees. From red squirrels? But the structure had no opening whereby something could pass in or out. Another mystery, and it added to the questions I often ask myself when passing through the grove. Like, why did some idiot plant these trees so close together that, in early days, I had to crawl inside them on all fours to start the pruning and cutting process? And why do I even bother with the work here, winter in and winter out?

Climbing the seasonal roadway toward the top of Dryden Hill, I left the personal domain behind. I left my baggage, so to speak, my problems and property, at the bottom of the hill. The summits out beyond have a life-force, even in winter, and I aimed to rediscover it. I sensed the life-force in the flight of birds—in the few ravens, crows, jays, and sparrows I encountered. It helped to sponge up the anxieties linked to human life while preparing me for something else. I felt ready to be taken over, mind and body, by some plant or animal or even by an oncoming storm. I spooked several deer at the roadway—and they bolted for the deep woods, perhaps recognizing the foibles I displayed.

I stopped: the tracks in the snow were new to me. I knelt by the fresh imprints and fumbled with my camera. Each track was two to three-inches long. Five toes were set symmetrically on each foot. The middle toe was slightly longer than the rest. Claw marks were clearly indicated in the snow. They were not left by red squirrel or raccoon, by fox or bobcat, by porcupine or opossum. Could they be a fisher's? I would have to do some research when I got back home. Fishers have been seen occasionally by town residents; and these large members of the weasel family have been photographed by trail-cam on the rivertops. I may have seen one, myself, a few months earlier.

Recharged, I scrambled upward through a tunnel formed by native pines. At the junction of two gravel roads I passed the old McKenna place, the farmhouse, barn, and former one-room schoolhouse. All was quiet here except for echoes in my head and the sudden arrival of wind. We valley folks forget, sometimes, how winter winds can rake voraciously across the summits, as if to seek out every insect, sparrow and grain from summer crops.

Greenwood township had installed a road sign here at 2,400 feet above sea-level. The sign warned of "Merging Traffic" at the junction I had passed. Yeah, I mused, traffic can be an issue here, enough to make a resident decry the vehicle or two that passes every day and make him want to move out to the *country*. On a clear day up on Dryden you can see for miles to the south and east. I've thought that, with luck, one might even see across the world and eventually glimpse the back side of one's head. On this day, however, the clouds looked heavy with the promise of snow; I couldn't see much beyond the wooded slopes of Bootleg Hollow. Somewhere down below me in the valley stood the old house where I live. Closer at hand lay the overgrown remnants of a cellar from a farmhouse stolen by the passage of perhaps a hundred years. The stone remnants hung about me like a specter, as if requiring the body of a house, a structure like my own place in the hollow.

I gave another glance at the hilltop across the valley and froze at the prospect of wind turbines soon to be erected on area summits. I had lived here too long and loved these rural scenes too much to wish for an invasion of industrial behemoths in my home. No matter how quickly man was causing global climate change, no matter how thoroughly the energy corporations white-washed the impacts they proposed, I had moved here to be free as possible from the urban overflow and from the evidence of our own destruction—I didn't need to see any 600-foot towers whirling their blades in my face.

I descended toward the hollow through a deep ravine in the woods. I thought of a warmer season and of fly-fishing the streams of home and places far away. My life was like a river, I supposed. My thoughts could subdivide life's river into smaller streams and waterways. In daydreams, I could see across a continent of beautiful waters that I could hike and fish along. Yes, I was anxious for a new season.

Returning to the margins of humanity, I paused to study several milkweed plants with pods split open to the winter breezes. Cloudy seeds clung to the pods like small birds on a nest awaiting flight. Inside my house again, I checked several resources and confirmed my hunch about the fisher tracks. A loping fisher has the track pattern that I clearly saw, suggesting that the front feet land in snow before the hind feet land, and that a backfoot steps inside the track laid by a front one. Each of the heels is a minimal thing, with the snow suggesting a C-shaped pad.

I thought back to the site where the tracks were found. I had hoped to follow the prints but lost them where the fisher had crossed a stream. It was good to have a spirit of the wild scoping out your home. I wished the hunter well, with plenty of red squirrels and porcupines (yes!) and maybe even a feral cat or two to keep it in the neighborhood.

2

With the air temperature registering a breezy 16 degrees Fahrenheit, it was too cold to fly-fish, but the prospect of an upriver hike seemed appealing.

The afternoon sun broke out sporadically from the clouds, and I was glad to be walking an abandoned railroad grade along the upper Allegheny River, protected from the wind that swept the hilltops. I was also sheltered from the sight and sounds of a hydrofracking operation on the slope above, where the work of mining for shale gas continues day and night.

I had just purchased my 31st consecutive non-resident fishing license for Pennsylvania waters. Although a sane attempt to fly-fish in this weather wouldn't be possible today (don't ask me to define a *sane* attempt at winter fly-fishing in the North), it was good to celebrate three decades of involvement with rivertop country by hiking toward the source of the Allegheny-Ohio-Mississippi watershed, beside one of our nation's longest rivers.

On the trail, I could feel the breath of wildness like a cool breeze through the layers of clothing on my back. Coyote tracks were printed freshly in the granular snow, and there again—the tracks of fisher, indisputable in an ice-bed of the Allegheny, paw-prints like coyote's but rounder and clearly punctuated with impressions of five long toes.

I could hike for several miles before nearing the highway to Gold, and I had time to think. I bought my first PA angling license in 1987, the year in which Michael Czarnecki and I were busy publishing and promoting the Upriver Poetry Chapbook Series, with works by Graham Duncan, Karen Blomain, Barbara Crooker, and Terry Keenan (FootHills Publishing and Great Elm Press). Shortly thereafter, I published an anthology of outdoor writers called *Riveries*, appropriately enough.

As time passed, I may have left the strict realms of poetry in favor of exploring the region's fly-fishing opportunities and writing of them in prose but, looking back, I don't see a separation as much as a merging of literary elements with the various aspects of outdoor recreation. Recently, here at Dryden Hill, I opened Barbara Crooker's chapbook, *Starting at Zero*, which we produced in 1987. I was stunned by several lines in the first poem, "January," that seemed connected to my Allegheny River hike: "… And here we are, poised on the rim of the year, / this icy globe turning. / We're caught in suspension, / our every breath visible. / The silence between us deepens,/ blue as the shadows in snow."

The lines returned me to the hike along the year's rim, listening to blue silence by the snowy headwaters of a very young river. I remembered reaching one of the uppermost trout pools in the Allegheny, a placid forest scene only a mile or so from the river's source, where I paused in thoughts about an unfinished poem. I'd recited the first lines of that unfinished piece at the gathering for my mother's memorial a week after her death at Christmas time. Those lines from "Poem, 2:30 A.M.": *She who brought me into this river of life/ brought me to a love/ of flowing waters...*

Returning to the Allegheny River point where I began the hike, I resolved to come fish here in the spring, when the native trout would be eager to take a dry fly on the surface, when the season has green eyes and breath, and is several months removed from the rim.

3

One year, on December 30, nearly all the streams and rivers of the region were flowing high and muddy from recent rains, but I found a head-waters stream manageable for fly-fishing. I was close to the source of one of the longest rivers on the continent and, for an hour or so, I was casting comfortably with a Glo-Bug in the cold, dark woods of northern Pennsylvania. I landed a wild brown trout, a finned spirit with striking color, and I practiced my winter angling, reabsorbing that slow-motion feel of working the rod and line with an occasional fish controlled (or uncontrolled) by half-frozen fingers, toes, and brain.

As the New Year dawned, Tim, a fishing partner, and I got together once again for our fourth consecutive fly-rod outing on the holiday, despite some challenging conditions. Our options in New York were limited due to closed seasons, snowy weather, and a lack of time, but we did okay, considering.

We chose a home-county stream that neither one of us had much experience with. We knew that Mill Creek had a reputation for good wild trout fishing—if you don't mind casting on a small stream through some tight, brushy corridors. It's an under-utilized fishery, at least by fly-casters, so we thought it might be fun. The weather reminded us of steelhead angling—when the big rainbows make their spawning run in winter or early spring. Then it's often cold and blustery, but this was New Year's Day. Tradition called, and we couldn't just ignore it.

I was up in one of those alder tunnels of Mill, in knee-deep water, when I hooked a fine brown. Removing my new pair of cheap Dollar General gloves, I stuck them between my knees while pulling in the trout. I quickly photographed the fish and let it go, but it slipped back to the roily water with a glove that loosened from between my knees. Departure happened so fast I didn't see the glove float away. Later, I told Tim about the fish, and asked if he had seen a black glove floating by. He hadn't seen the fugitive article, but said, "It sounds like the trout might have stolen it!"

A gremlin, a rascally salmonid, could have taken the glove. If so, no amount of winter practice on my part could have prevented the theft. The trout would have had some New Year design of its own, although whatever use it could have had for a glove is more than I can fathom. Then again, trout can steal greater things from anglers, can't they? Things like dreams and imagination.

Soon we met a fellow who was possibly the world's sorriest spin-fisherman, a guy who had just come from a deep ravine on Mill. Giving him credit for venturing out on a cold day, we approached him just to say hello and to ask if he knew of more fishing access on the creek. The angler was young and had driven a new pickup truck to Mill. It seemed that he had reasons for being optimistic about life but, responding to our pleasantries, he merely grunted and continued toward the parking lot.

S*omething* had stolen that angler's sense of human worth, and it's doubtful that the culprit was a trout. Even if he had just hooked and lost a massive trout in the ravine, he would have come out with a smile and a shake of the head. But no, a wild fish seldom steals a human soul. It wasn't likely that we'd find another angler that unfriendly in the upcoming year, not while casting flies on our favorite waters. As another trout or two came to our frozen hands that day, it seemed as if these fishes from the good Earth gave us more than just a look at their winter skins. They gave us a gift, of sorts, something to be shared in future days.

4

In a cold season here on Dryden Hill, I was looking back to a warmer and more colorful period, a recent autumn when I fished the headwaters and was led to none other than the European explorer, Columbus. Sure, he was a modern-day Columbus, a guy I met on "Columbus Day," but nonetheless...

I began the long weekend by fishing a couple of trout streams in northern Pennsylvania. I was suiting up at a mountain crossroad near Cedar Run when Columbus came roaring at me on a motorcycle. He glared as he approached and brought his Harley to an idling pause. The biker looked like a city cop in his helmet and black-leather uniform; and to think of him as Columbus I had to acknowledge myself as an unknown nature writer rather than pretending to be Richard Brautigan, author of *Trout Fishing in America*.

My subject wasn't some sea-faring dude who's lost his way beneath the scattering stars. This free-wheeling explorer extricated his GPS from who knows where and started tapping at keys... "How do you spell Cedar?" he asked. "C-e-a-d... No," he mumbled, talking directly at the unit.

"Cedar," I stated, "C-e-d-a-r. Look there, on the road sign. Cedar Run. *That* way."

"It's telling me I should go... this direction. Where's that lead to?" asked Columbus.

"Leetonia. You can go that way, but you can also take this road," I indicated, pointing to the road signs once again. "Toward Marshlands. Then take a left on Cedar Mountain Road. It's a nice day to *get lost*, isn't it?"

"A beautiful day," replied Columbus, with the early morning sunlight brightening over his head, and with the forest leaves blazing into multi-colored hue. "Okay, I'll try this road." He blasted away on his two-wheeled mission. But before I could get my wading shoes laced up tightly, he came roaring back down the mountain road and passed me at the intersection, shouting, "Why the *hell* doesn't this *work*?"

Columbus zoomed back the way he'd come originally, on the road to Colton Point, but it might as well have been the route to Portugal. Before I had my cane rod strung together for some fishing nearby, I could hear him returning, a man with a job to do, looking for an India-of-the-Mind, motoring through the circles on his mental map then shooting outward on the one road yet untaken—the trail to Marshlands, with a left to Cedar Run.

I could then fish in the deep woods of a blue October day, alone on a sparkling brook trout stream, almost as if Columbus had never existed. And that's the thing about cold, clear, flowing water. It sweeps a prospect of the marvelous to your feet and ankles and your vision of the world. It can mesh your soul with the grandeur and the force of the beyond. It can bring Columbus or Napoleon or Amelia Earhart to your head. It helps to energize us through imagination—birds in flight upon the sea, small beings capable of recognizing our own urges in a world where multiplicity and diversity define reality and truth. But that's a boat-load of significance, a great burden maybe, that we place on flowing water in a lovely corner of the world. To lighten the load, I almost expected to find graffiti scratched boldly on the rock walls near my stream: "Columbus was here, October 2015."

At that point I began to muse on how my daughter would be leaving soon for a new life on a Caribbean island. We'd be wishing her well and hoping that the U.S. Virgin Islands were Columbus free. My wife and I would soon be taking Alyssa to the Rochester airport for her flight to St. Croix. My home river, the Genesee, flows through Rochester just before it enters Lake Ontario, and since I'd never fished that lower stretch for trout or salmon, I thought I'd take the opportunity to introduce myself before sending off Alyssa on her flight.

Autumn trout and great Pacific salmon swim up to the Lower Falls in Rochester to spawn, and if you hit the river at the right time, you can have extraordinary fishing, so I've heard. If ever I was going to feel like Columbus might have felt when realizing he was blown off course, it was going to happen there and then…

The Genesee River Gorge was beautiful with autumn's brightest colors, but the river was wide, muddy and filled with impossible rocks. The bank fishermen were numerous. In the places where I typically fly-fish, almost all the people I encounter are white. Minorities (and women anglers) are seldom seen, unfortunately. But fishing in the city, downstream of the Lower Falls, changed all that for me.

I looked out of place, but I felt fine. Blacks, Latinos, and women of all races could be found there on a late October afternoon. Granted, I don't like crowds when I fish, but with this new diversity of anglers, I didn't mind so much. Most of the people looked poor; the Orvis gang seemed worlds away. A couple of old guys, casting live bait or corn or Cleos with a spinning rod, asked if they could have my fish, in case I didn't want them.

I had little chance of catching a fish here with a fly, although I saw some huge ones breaching the water well beyond my casting range. I don't know what Columbus would have done if he was fishing here, but I was thinking to relinquish my usual catch-and-release ethos if I should land a legal fish. I would give it away to someone who could use it.

I remembered the few readings I'd be giving at local libraries from my newly published book. I could daydream that Columbus had read about a future reading and decided to attend. Wow, I was somehow worthy of his attentions! He would stand around at the reading, listening or pretending to be interested. He would even buy a copy of my book and ask if I would sign it for him. "Sure," I'd say. "I'll sign it for you." And this is what I'd write:

"To Columbus... Thanks for rediscovering America... October, 2015..." Yours in exploration.

5

With the ease of a daydream from the comfort of home, I could drift back from these winter hills to a spring day on the water. I could feel useful again, assisting my Trout Unlimited chapter with a clean-up project on a headwater stream...

Over a period of several days, we had gathered two large dumpster-loads of garbage from a feeder of the upper Genesee. We worked like demented demi-gods in beautiful weather, pulling heavy trash from a deep ravine. Taking our punishment like Sisyphus, we rolled tires uphill (some of them on the metal rim) on a pipeline right-of-way at a 40-degree angle. We'd push a tire uphill to the road, walk back down for another tire, and another, till I felt like I'd been pulling bald tires forever.

We told ourselves (unconvincingly) that fishing would suck on a blue-sky morning like this, that the work was necessary and inevitable. The Green Drake nymphs would sleep in beds of river silt, unable to rise and hatch, because the sun was too damned bright. The trout would be sleeping-in, as well, although a few fish might suspect that the boys were out collecting trash, so it might be fun to swim around and eat some bugs.

Gathering disposable diapers was a cheerless task but walking the forested brookie waters where thrushes fluted softly was a treat. To reward myself for volunteer service, I soon went fishing in north-central Pennsylvania.

I came to a creek that has a roadside trailer camp named "We Tried." The name is painted on a head-board just above the doorway of this faded and perhaps forgotten camp. Each time that I've passed the place in the many years I've fished nearby, I've had to chuckle at the name... We Tried. I was reminded of the way that many people try to reconnect with the wildness of their dreams. And then I came to J.R.'s farm...

The old farm contains about a mile of excellent trout stream. Several outdoor writers have described this stream where J.R. dwells as one of the best wild fisheries in the state. The stream is made sweeter by the fact that relatively few people fish it, other than on the lower sections that have stocked trout and public access. The upper portions are managed for wild trout production, and that's where I was headed. The browns in J.R.'s mile of water would be eager for a hatch of late-May Sulphurs, Grey Fox, Green Drakes, and the spinner forms of these emergent insects.

Mac's Pool, which I named for J.R.'s grandson, was the hotspot on the stream again. Mac, a young middle-schooler with a keen interest in all things angling, had caught a 26-inch brown trout in the pool a year ago. He had proudly posed with his catch for a photo that eventually appeared in the county newspaper.

In the evening as I stood in Mac's Pool I could hear a heavy trout slap the surface for a mayfly dun. The sound was a pleasant distraction from my thoughts about Mac's bait-fishing attempts—from the sight of his ungodly mess of hooks and line and sinkers wound around the branches overhead. A month earlier I had lost a large trout, perhaps the same one I could hear feeding at the surface, when it took my fly and leader into the stumps adjacent to the pool. Perhaps Mac could've horsed the big fish with his 8-pound monofilament, but my 5x tippet wouldn't hold.

Anyway, the duns and spinners blanketed the evening water. I had several good fish on the line, all of them spitting out the hook, before I became successful. Perhaps I'd had the big trout on the line, as well, but in the fervor of the rise, it was difficult to know. Like the fellas who had owned a hunting and fishing camp nearby, I tried. Yeah, I tried.

A Stream of Dreams

1

There seems to be a lot of literature pertaining to crafted walking sticks, and a lot of information can be found that deals with the availability of commercialized walking instruments. I'll confess to having read very little of the walking-stick brochures available and have been deficient in boosting the economy by purchasing crafted sticks of soulless quality.

I'll accept the fact that Ben Franklin gave his favorite walker to George Washington and that it's now a national treasure. I have no problem believing that sticks can be family heirlooms and collectibles worth money. For me, however, the walking stick is a practical item, a natural tool to help me get somewhere outdoors and to better appreciate the place I'm in. It helps me to better understand that place and guide me toward whatever goal I have in mind, to focus on simply getting there.

The walking stick is an extension of my outdoor self, no less important than binoculars to a birder or fishing rods to an angler. My sticks range from a beaver-chewed alder staff to a crooked sassafras pole to a "systems" stick that I'll refer to later. I use them as supporters and shields, as tools to pick up trash, or simply as an item that feels good and elemental in the hand. The stick can also function as a pointer—an attention grabber for a trail mate too self-absorbed to see the interesting wildflower or the migratory bird that he or she was about to shuffle past.

A walking stick was possibly mankind's first defense weapon and support tool. Early specimens were as friendly as a shepherd's crook or as fearsome as a pike or spear. We can still imagine them being whittled on an Appalachian porch. We can shape them into being from a suitable branch that's fallen near a trail-head. High-technology has produced synthetic canes, as well, some of which have medical applications for physical infirmities.

My own preference is for a beaver-cut aspen or poplar stick about four-feet long. I have several of these and am always looking for another when I'm close to beaver dams and lodges. My favorite stick has the bark removed by rodent teeth. It's knotty in convenient locations and is tapered to a slightly bent tip. It's great for bushwhacking maneuvers. The wood is soft but light and durable. There's a feeling of resiliency and life to it, and the stick slides readily through the hand when I want it to.

I also own a manufactured "systems stick" that my late mother-in-law once gave me as a gift. Only in America can you find an item like this (although it may have been manufactured overseas)—a four-sided piece of finished hickory with a knob on top.

It's endowed with a compass that glows at night, with a wrist-cord and a retractable spike that's good for wading, trash collection, and emergency hunting and fishing ventures. The stick has a rubber tip, plus an ingenious device for measuring the height of distant trees and buildings. Similar productions, I am told, might come with such necessities as sundials, swords, microscopes, and skinny violins. No doubt the sword or the violin could soothe the beast found on a mountaintop, but I'm still trying to fathom the application of sundials and microscopes in such locales.

I hardly ever use my systems stick, and I haven't yet explored its possibilities doubling as aerobic exerciser, camera mono-pod, scale, and "thumper"—the latter being useful to ward off grizzlies, feral dogs and serial killers. The instruction manual for this stick includes the caveat not to use on toothy mammals larger than yourself unless you can aim straight, throw hard, and run like a cheetah. Again, my preference is to use the simpler rodent sticks discovered near the water.

An ordinary walking stick helps me get past all the gizmos and most of the nonsense in our lives. It helps me reach my stream of dreams, my wild free-flowing rush of water where reality and dream converge and almost coincide.

2

Before Chris Peterson, a local journalist, left western New York to live in Montana, he published a list of his favorite wild trout streams in my region.

Each stream got a few words from Peterson's own fishing experiences. One brook, especially, was said to be "like walking into the past." I took these words to heart, thinking the place sounded like fun, and yes, I found the little stream to be intriguing. It was like going to meet God on his original stomping ground and being asked to decide, there and then, if you were going to become a believer or remain an atheist or agnostic.

The small stream had a wild ambience and yielded several large brown trout near the headwaters, fish that I presumed were living on smaller native trout for sustenance. A few days later, however, I revisited the brook at a downstream site and had a rough time of it. The water was low, clear and cold, with distracting sights—discarded tires, plastic bottles, and glimpses of a house or a cabin. I had walked into a different version of the past. The daydreams of a pristine landscape had changed into the reality of a stream where God's house was disheveled, with bits of garbage and intrusions from the human world.

I moved on to another tributary of the upper Genesee River, this one even more remote and forested than the previous brook. Again, I had the fly rod with me as I "walked into the past"—if the past included stories of rural residents dumping garbage into ravines, of people who found it easier to toss waste into a convenient gully rather than disposing of it properly. Several years earlier I had organized a major clean-up of this stream with Trout Unlimited and county residents who care about the land and its waters.

I would catch a few wild trout at this location where the young leeks greened the slopes nearby and where clusters of spring beauty and hepatica starred the banks. God wasn't near the place, as far as I could tell, but his tracks were there, or so I imagined.

I caught up with Him at a third stream in the headwaters. Here, where Trout Unlimited has made a positive impact in recent years, I imagined that God was hanging around to look things over. I was pleased to be here on a beautiful, sparkling stream. I felt like I had walked back to a time and place where God and human might converse together while casting flies or other lures for trout. I imagined a friendly dual with God, a game called "One Fly, Maybe Two." I chose a Gold-ribbed Hare's Ear pattern, with a Hendrickson nymph as back-up. God selected a Black Stonefly nymph with a Grannom wet fly as a second pattern for the day. We could use no other flies.

God had home-field advantage in our little angling contest. He approached his first pool carefully and tried his hand before saying, "Okay, your turn." We went back and forth, stalking upstream through each pool and riffle, no one better than the other, looking forward to earning points scored for each trout captured and released.

As the mid-day heat began to wear me down, I started thinking about the prize that the loser would bestow upon the better angler—a case of assorted craft beers from a local brewery. If I won, I also had the option of telling God exactly what I thought of Him without concern for any consequence.

The daydream didn't go quite as planned. God lost his Stonefly on a backcast into a tree. He replaced it with his Grannom and began to fuss about the leader tippet. I grew impatient. God then made a cast into one of the finest runs along the stream and hooked another full-bodied brook trout. I knew the game was up. "You win," I said reluctantly. "I'm buying."

"No," said God. "I'm just starting to enjoy this thing. If you quit now, you won't like the consequences."

"W-what do you mean, God? I said I quit!"

"Okay. I'm the winner, but I don't want your beer. Go up to that bend pool and look closely at the streambank... People are such ignoramuses."

I had no foresight of the stream's sharp bend but what I found there sliced my solitude as if with a knife. I saw a rusty leg-hold trap wired to a root exposed from an undercut of the bank. The trap, probably from an autumn or winter setting now forgotten by some hunter of furs, held a rotten leg with flesh and bone still weaving in the water currents. The trapper had never bothered coming back to check his line. But what did God have to do with this? Did my presence with Him mean that we were all ignoramuses, but that some could believe in travel toward a stream of dreams, to a place where we could make a real change in ourselves or in the world?

I checked the remnant of a carcass to see what species of life had been held there in the jaws of steel. The paw told the story of raccoon. The dark

flesh resembled a tiny hand. The game was
certainly over.

3

I found the heavy *touchstone* many years ago,
perhaps in a gravel pit near an Indian burial ground;
I can't be sure. It was probably a Native American
artifact. I think I found it on a piece of land about to
be converted into New York's section of Interstate
86 when construction happened in the early 1970s.
The stone might have been used initially as a tool
for tightening and drying animal skins. A hole had
been drilled through the rock. There's a ridge line
on the stone dividing each end of the long hole and
appearing to give it a facial characteristic. The
smooth rock with its odd shape is a touchstone for
me, but not in the usual sense. I don't use it to
determine a standard for stones; I don't strike it
with another rock to determine the quality of
minerals. I simply touch it and allow my
imagination to roam.

Touchstone is a clownish character in
Shakespeare's "As You Like It," a comedy I read
long ago in high school. Touchstone is the wise fool
who can play with language and the power of
words, who can guide the drama and put himself
and all other characters to the comic test. He's a
touchstone of another stripe and color.

With his assistance, I allow myself to make
connections and associations. For example, I think
about a large millipede I found last summer
crawling on a mountain in New Mexico. The

millipede becomes more than just a curious animal. With help from the touchstone I can ask the millipede questions like, "Do you miss the cottonwoods while you're hiking under the desert sun?" To us, it might sound magical, or foolish, but if I can get an answer from a millipede, it's probably springing up, originally, from that Touchstone character, the Fool of Arden.

Recently I found the *usnea* plant behind my house among dead apple trees. Usnea might be considered a touchstone from the floral kingdom. Usnea is the genus name for several species of lichen that hang from trees. It grows like a clump of gray or greenish hair on my decaying orchard. Other common names for the plant are beard lichen, tree moss, and old man's beard. In learning about this plant, I remembered Tolkien's character, Treebeard, oldest of the Ents. I might be going out on a limb in saying this (pun intended), but usnea is my touchstone for the magical blends of lichen and algae.

Usnea grows slowly on sick or dying trees where an opened canopy allows it to photosynthesize more readily. Sensitive to air pollution, especially to sulphur dioxide, the plant was once widespread and luxuriant in Great Britain where it now appears to have been decimated in most locales other than the highlands. Usnea has a reputation for healing certain afflictions. It contains a great deal of vitamin C. For a thousand years or more, it was thought to contain what's now considered to be antibiotic and antifungal agents. Usnea was applied internally as well as topically.

Viewing my dying apple trees that hold a few clumps of usnea, I thought of Treebeard and his friends. At one point in *The Lord of the Rings*, the tree-like Ents decide to attack the forces of Suruman in retaliation for destroying their forest and using the plunder for war. I thought the Ents would make a wonderful ally in the fight against environmental degradation here at home and in other places of the world.

Usnea is used for nesting by a colorful warbler known as the Northern Parula. This blue and yellow songbird has been extirpated from some of its northern range (as in New York State). The population decrease may be due, in part, to changes in the warbler's habitat, perhaps because of air pollution that inhibits the growth of lichens necessary for its nest construction.

As a touchstone, usnea is an ordering device, a tool. It provides a moment of peace when I contemplate its origins. The madness of civilization falls away briefly then. It's like a quick vacation in Shakespeare's Arden. I like it when Touchstone plays with words and blends a black-and-white reality with the limitless beyond. Nature provides a gift, a vision of perfection, like the trout stream where the dream of fishing with ideal conditions almost coincides with the reality of the water itself.

Man-made objects can have a similar effect. I recently tied some Hare's Ear wet flies and found myself dreaming productively, "Far away, yet close to home." I tied the classic Hare's Ear on large hooks with a bead-head up in front. Nothing complicated here. The pattern's been around since

1839 or earlier, and British fly-fishing literature suggests that it was tied with fur pulled from between the long ears of a hare.

Is it a hare's mask that I see in the contours of my gravel-pit stone? Does the image lend itself to the somber trout-fly pattern loved by anglers far and wide? Never flashy, this great imitator of trout foods, this touchstone of the wet fly realm, often becomes more effective when it frays and looks a bit disheveled.

The Hare's Ear is a standard-bearer of the fly box. I tie it and see a rainbow leaping from a river on the far side of the nation. The trout could be leaping from a pristine river in a corner of Wyoming, a remote and picturesque location rarely visited by fishermen or tourists. It's a wonderful place, if only in the mind. Technically, the river could be ripping from a mountaintop, too high and muddy from the melting snow to take an angler's line. Its blackflies and mosquitoes could be too voracious for the casual visitor; the river road could be closed out by an avalanche; who knows for sure? Only the river knows the depth that time hopes to reveal. It flows onward, gathering force and balance in the daydreams of a naturalist. I see its beauty in a newly-tied Hare's Ear clutched in the iron jaws of a tightened vise. I see its bed-rock in a touchstone cradled in the hand.

4

To say I go "fishing with antiques", I'm not referring to a rendezvous with other geezers like myself. Rather, I sometimes try to slow the hectic pace of life and, by doing so, immerse myself in a stream of dreams with old *equipment* close at hand. Old, as in a 1930s rod and reel. Old, as in casting a lightweight F.E. Thomas bamboo rod attached to a Hardy Uniqua reel. Some guys like to buffer up an old '57 Chevy alongside their latest pickup truck; I enjoy a chance to use a bit of classic fishing tackle.

I mostly save the use of old equipment for special occasions, although a recent hot day in early summer didn't seem particularly meritorious. Weather forecasters suggested we might be seeing a period of hot, dry days, meaning that the New York fishing season could be facing a major slump. If so, I'd better go fishing one more time, at least, and make it count.

I have more than my share of modern fishing equipment but there's something reassuring about the use of older stuff, i.e., those well-kept glass and bamboo rods and classic-era reels. The older tools that I employ were mostly purchased second-hand over the years and they amount to what was standard tackle for the first half of the 1900s. I find that angling traditions beckon in this modern day and age. Although I like my angling methodology to be progressive, always seeking new horizons of experience, I also enjoy the history and traditions of the fly-fishing sport. A hand-crafted rod or reel from the so-called golden age of fly-fishing, or a well-made instrument from contemporary artisans reflecting the classic era, is a fine thing to behold. Today I chose to go with a Thomas rod and a Hardy winch. I could've ventured out with a silk fly line, too, but didn't want to deal with that on this occasion.

My 8-foot 6-inch F. E. Thomas rod is the company's "Maine Special." This Thomas model isn't signed by the builder, but it has his signature wrap of silk threads above the cork handle of the rod. This fly rod isn't one of the maker's higher-grade models, but it is in good condition and is fun to cast. Thomas, once an apprentice to the venerable bamboo rod craftsman, H. L. Leonard, began to build rods independently in the early 1900s and produced some of the finest split-cane instruments ever. I once owned one of his better fly rods, a "Bangor" model that I used for steelhead and salmon, that eventually was traded for a different bamboo rod. My old Maine Special is a 5-weight that has intermediate silk windings and a slight over-varnish. The Uniqua reel by Hardy has a soft, fluttery, metallic click that's almost comforting as I turn the handle. There are any number of wonderful pieces out there of a similar grade, or much better, that can help one set up on the stream of dreams. It doesn't take much money to get there, either, if you set priorities, and maybe scrimp a little on the so-called luxuries of life. Old tackle from a reputable dealer can do wonders for the inquisitive angler. The trick lies in how we approach that stream of dreams, in how the mind and body cast their line.

In real life, I didn't get on the river till 8 a.m., rather late for a day whose temperature was slated to peak at the 90-degree mark. I should have been there at daybreak. I immediately noticed a trout rise to an emerging insect but decided to begin by casting a dry fly, a Blue-winged Olive, for tradition's sake, even though my chances for success beneath a bright sky weren't too good. I did it for the fun of casting with a fly that I could follow on the water, to spite, for once, whatever science or decorum was involved, to be lazy on a warming day, because I could.

I didn't have any luck, so after a while I changed my ways and started working. I experimented with various small fly patterns, from caddis emergers to Blue Quill spinners to Ants, but the trout weren't interested. I started working on my casts—the far and fine to the short cast with a specified location in mind. Hooking up became a secondary consideration. I thought about the old rod and reel and how these pieces fit my expectation here. I thought about the wood duck hen and her cluster of chicks that scuttled from my slow approach to the stream, about the cedar waxwings and the great-crested flycatcher fluttering from the branches overhead. The moments felt timeless, somehow fragile yet resilient, like a mayfly wing.

5

As America approached yet another Independence Day celebration, I was reminded that occasionally a chance encounter while fishing will unveil an interesting portrait of human freedom.

I had been fishing the caddis hatch on the upper Genesee, walking upstream in a clear and comfortable evening, when glancing toward a bend pool I could see a fly line flowing back and forth while also hearing soft words spoken as if to a son or a fishing buddy. It took several minutes before I could clearly view the bearded fellow—a big man with glasses who appeared to be about my age. The partner he'd been talking to, even while landing a trout, was a lively little terrier.

As we approached each other, I saw that the small dog carried a bag of angling paraphernalia by holding two straps in its mouth. I said, "Oh, you've got your helper with you tonight," and the fly-fisher, John B., replied with "Yeah, she's my ghillie."

We exchanged fishing reports, and I learned that John B. likes to fly-cast on the headwaters of streams, as I do, way up in what he calls "the nose-bleed section." The headwaters is often the place where no one else is found, unless one chances on another madman or iconoclast in love with native trout.

John fishes the wilder streams of New York and Pennsylvania and he knows many of my favorites such as Slate and Cedar Run. He fishes them remotely, "where you can die of dehydration and exhaustion if you go in with a bloated ego and aren't prepared for canyon walking."

One of John B.'s fishing heroes was Fran Betters, but he knew him only late in life, when the Ausable River shopkeeper had to sit while fishing or when tying Adirondack patterns at his vise. "Nowadays I like to sit on my ass while fishing, like Fran had to do," said John. I politely reminded him that it isn't easy to sit down while investigating rivertops like these.

John and his canine companion were about to leave and head back to the parking lot when he said, "Oh wait, I've got a story you'll appreciate." It went something like this…

"One time I was fishing near the state hatchery on Oswayo Creek—you know, Potter County. I saw a guy fishing who acted like he didn't want anyone to know what he was up to. I walked over and saw a fly rod getting tossed into the grass. He tore off his vest and tried to chuck that, too, but four or five cans of Falstaff Beer fell out to the edge of the creek by the hatchery. Christ, I couldn't believe a guy would drink that shit. Falstaff! Anyhow, this guy looked totally embarrassed and we finally introduced ourselves. Are you ready for this? The fellow was none other than …." John supplied the name of a legendary Pennsylvania fly-fisher, writer, and angling partner of former President Jimmy Carter. "It was the only time I ever met the man!"

I've got a new name for the bend pool where I found John B. I'm calling it the Rabbit Hole, in honor of Alice and her entry into Wonderland. After meeting this angler, I had a stronger appreciation of what Alice dealt with in her journeys.

Before John B. left, I asked him where he lives and what he does when not out fishing in the nose-bleed section. I learned that he lives in the Genesee watershed, and that he takes great pleasure in reading books and making music. "I don't have a TV, cell phone or computer," he said. "I just read and make CDs. About 100 of them so far."

A hundred albums? I nearly fell in the water. "Do you write songs?" I asked.

"No… well, sometimes. About my friends, like this dog here. I've been featured on Dr. Demento. Stuff like that."

Dr. Demento… John wanted to know which vehicle on the parking lot was mine, so he could leave some sample CDs for me. Later, when I left the Rabbit Hole and got back to the car at dusk, I found four self-produced albums waiting for me. I played one of them while driving home. I wasn't done with my Wonderland experience yet.

The albums are remarkable, bizarre, completely wild but focused. "Songs and Legends of Allegany County" (Genesee River country) is satirical, hilarious, original. The albums are full of local history and an independent spirit. John Bartles, the angler, and his Diode Trio should have a major recording label, but we can rest assured the band will never get one. As John told me on the river, this is rough-and-tumble music. No-holds-barred. Unsuited for ANY age, but totally enjoyable, whether you're listening to John's more serious work or to the stuff that, by design, makes no point at all. The Diode Trio has some You Tube offerings that work as an introduction to its Halls of *Academentia*.

Freedom is a wonderful thing when you have it. Freedom is a stream of dreams no dam can stop.

My Life in the Understory

Every man, by the very nature of life, is engaged in a struggle... to find his way back to perfect human sight. Man is not a sinner—he is a weary traveler lost under the hill, a material specter looking for his spiritual emanation.

– William Blake

1

While helping to clean the banks of a trout stream in northern Pennsylvania, I discovered several blossoms of the locally rare wildflower known as yellow lady's-slipper. I featured this flower on my nature blog without being overly site-specific and had an interesting response from an area wildlife conservation officer who enjoys photography and wildflowers.

The officer wondered where the yellow lady's-slipper could be found and photographed. If I didn't mind disclosing the location, he would go there in the hope of getting photographs while swearing secrecy about the flowers' whereabouts. I was glad to tell him of the site, and the officer was truly grateful for the wild connection and the opportunity to expand his flower and wildlife albums.

The lady's-slipper helped rekindle my own interest in our native flora and inspired me to revisit nearby Keeney Swamp before I ventured on the fishing road again. To find the *pink* lady's-slipper (Moccasin Flower) again, or the rarer wild orchids in Keeney Swamp, would be a highlight of my season. I entered the Keeney Swamp preserve and rambled through the drier sections of its 2,400-acres. Although I didn't find the rarer orchids, I managed to stumble on some fascinating plants including painted trillium, starflower and bunchberry.

The spring foliage had thickened overhead, and my eyes were mostly focused on the ground. A black bear crossed my path, and my camera was too slow to capture the shuffling bruin before it vanished in the understory. All I got for my attempt at a picture was a two-legged blur.

I gave thanks to the wildflowers—bunchberry, trillium, starflower—for not running away from me like the bear. I enjoy life in the understory of the swamp— the birds, the fish, the four-legged animals—and life beyond it in the hills and on the streams because these places seem ephemeral and dignified. An acquaintance with the wild in all its diversity is something that a soul requires for satisfaction and fulfillment.

A recent article in *Science* magazine made a case for humankind and its involvement in "The Sixth Great Extinction." The diversity of life on Earth is facing a sixth major annihilation, according to this view. It probably won't happen in entirety any time soon, but it's happening piece-meal, day by day, by habitat destruction, climate change, pollution—by ways in which we shape the sad course of our destiny.

The Fifth Extinction of life is known scientifically as the time when the dinosaurs vanished following the impact of a giant meteor on Earth, or possibly from a process of progressive volcanism. The Sixth Extinction, whereby species are allegedly dying at a rate of one-hundred to one-thousand times faster than before the rise of modern man, is marked by the effects we have on our planet. It's not because we humans are inherently good or evil, it's because we humans do what humans do.

The news of this extinction wasn't new to me. For many years (since I stopped fretting about the Bomb and learned to live in its shadow), my greatest fear, the one I first heard about from poet Gary Snyder, has been the drying of the gene pool on this planet and the slow diminishment of life's diversity. It's enough to make me want to get out there each day and learn the fascinating plants and animals while I can, and to understand what it is we're losing.

The bunchberry of the northern forest floor is both attractive and deceiving. What appears to be four white petals of a ground-hugging flower are *bracts*, or specialized leaves for a plant related to the dogwood tree. The bracts attract the human eye searching for late-spring flowers. They attract pollinators to the hub of the plant which, in this case, is a cluster of tiny green flowers otherwise unnoticed and unfertilized.

Like the starflower, painted trillium and so much more, the bunchberry plant allows me to see a share of evolution in the understory of the greening forest. At a time when a rambler like myself is having difficulty seeing what was clear and open just a few short weeks ago, it's good to look at a flower closely. Those four white bracts are not unlike a mirror or a clear pool in a stream. They lead you to the center of the bloom, the flower of yourself within. From there it's possible to envision the long river of one's life.

2

The first morning of summer vacation seemed like a good time for a walk. I gathered some tools of the trade—camera, walking stick, water flask, small rod and reel—and took off for the hill.

I climbed on new ground for a while, to the summer fields and forest that drew me like the hive that had drawn the honeybees in my yard. I felt free to roam and contemplate the places of my long-time home, locations held tightly in my body like a swarm of thoughts and daydreams. Carl, our knowledgeable apiarist, had removed a swarm of bees from a birch tree in my yard, perhaps at a moment when the scout bees were still at work investigating possibilities for a new home on this hill. The old hive, in a fixture of our attic, had felt the pressures of a growing population and produced a new queen when the weather seemed right. When Carl stepped carefully into the birch tree to collect the swarm, shaking bees into a basket then pouring them into his box, you could almost hear the spirit of the hive, an energy like the human mind at work.

I pushed on through the forest and emerged on the summit fields. A vast acreage of chest-high timothy rolled in waves, the wind undulating every surface in the area. Titmice chattered at the wood's edge; a bluebird warbled from a dead tree near an old stone wall, and bobolinks spangled a separate meadow with their song.

Far down valley to the north I could see that showers were approaching. I reentered the familiar woods, secure in the knowledge that even if the sky darkened suddenly and the winds blew with horrendous power, I could find my way home without the use of compass, map or digital device. I had "scout bees" telling me to relax, that all of this was home—the points of field and forest, hill and valley, earth and sky, all adding up to the heart of nature.

It was dark and quiet in the hemlock woods. A late-morning thrush sang from a hidden post. A gray fox bounded off without a sound. I came to the clearing with its pond. There the bullfrogs leapt from cattail rafts; agitated redwings made direct flights at me, and I pieced together the small rod and reel that I had carried.

I caught and released some of the smallest sunfish on the planet. I did not expect or want anything more. The wind stirred the reeds; the sun and clouds brought on an endless array of miniature reflections. I imagined that honeybees lived in a dead tree by the pond.

Such is the spirit of a place. Alive in our heads, alive even when we're absent from the world outside.

3

Beavers had moved into the neighborhood. Although the beaver is increasingly abundant on many eastern waterways, the great rodent hasn't been seen much on the stream near my home, till recently.

The presence of beaver dams on eastern trout streams that are marginalized by human activity can be detrimental to the health of cold-water fishes. I don't mind the beavers' presence here on Bootleg Hollow Creek, however, because native trout have been sadly absent from its waters for 40 years or more. With some luck, the beavers' engineering might even enhance the microcosm of the small stream environment. A newly formed reservoir on the creek has encouraged a belted kingfisher to take up residence, and a green heron has arrived as well.

After photographing the industrious beavers one recent evening, I climbed the South Ridge just beyond the creek. I hadn't visited the old hemlock grove in several years and was hoping that its hermit thrushes were in vocal mode. They were. I love standing in forest solitude when these songsters, along with neighboring wood thrushes, pipe their territorial outcries in what seems like stereophonic splendor. I could never describe these intricate thrush songs, but I know that their notes and modulated phrasing add a deep mystery and enchantment to the summer woods.

I love the deep woods for the way the forest brings the ego to its knees, and for the way it reconstructs a balance in the seeker of solitude, the wanderer who needs to see the wild resurface in his or her life. I love the deep woods for the magic that's imparted there, and for the hint of danger, too. The act of balancing the wild and the civil elements within the self may be only short-lived but, if tumbling water sings of rocky passages or the wind strums its way across the hemlock boughs, the balance there is real.

Like the beaver and a multitude of upland creatures, the hermit thrush is home-keeping and doing what it must to survive. Come to think of it, we humans (most of us, at least) are doing something similar. After more than three decades in this place, I'm still trying to stake my ground here like a beaver or a thrush, still trying to write or to sing of it as my home.

A home is the place where your life feels right. It's a framework that extends beyond the body and gives meaning to the heart. It's a place as small as an apartment or as large as the globe. It's a place worthy of our songs and praises. It's organic and ever changing, a place that a thrush will sing of in the hemlock trees, a place that I'll try to write of in an essay or a poem.

Descending into the valley I re-crossed the flowing water and thought about a different stream not far away. It's a trout stream that forms a rivertop beyond a ridge near home. Lately I've been fly-fishing that stream and found that its native trout are doing well. The brook trout population has rebounded from a low point of several years ago, from an ebb apparently due to the rapid growth of the competitive brown trout population in the middle section of the creek.

Today it seems that the brook trout has the upper hand again. The creek changes dramatically year by year, sometimes due to man's activity, sometimes due to the stream itself and its response to changes in the weather. The creek's environmental issues stem largely from land abuse and invasive species, and at this point doesn't need an influx of beaver.

The beaver, an engineer of the first order, is a mammal whose controlling predators have been largely eradicated by humans. Thus, it becomes a creature that can negatively impact marginal trout streams in the eastern U.S.

There are no guarantees what tomorrow brings, of course, but for now I welcome the arrival of the beaver near my home. The animal is amazing, and it's good to have it in the neighborhood, especially if it temporarily ignores recovering waterways. Looking at the greater picture and considering the web of life as I understand it, the beaver has seniority here. It may even have more right to this place than I have. It's possible that we just might get along.

4

It seems that at least once a year I'll take a winter bath, swamping to my neck while hoisting the fly rod over my head, or grabbing for my hat before it floats down-river toward the bay. My most recent tumble into the cold drink occurred on a small stream in the state forest when the clear flow was high from recent rains.

I had stepped into a braid of water near a beaver dam that looked to be only knee-deep but had a silty bottom that collapsed and sucked me in. If there's any justice in this understory of mishaps and discovery, then the wild trout that I've taken and released there over time enjoyed a good laugh as I floundered on my back. Those fish may have heard me trying to annunciate a four-letter expletive to every bird and beaver in the neighborhood. And I don't care what anybody says—water can pour into waist-high waders, no matter how tightly a belt secures one's nether regions. My old billfold is still drying out.

Although the air temperature was slowly rising toward the 40s that day, I slogged back through the fields and woodland to the car feeling soggy, frozen and as hopeless as a Halloween spirit busted for decorating sidewalks with shaving cream and toilet paper.

I drove straight home to the warmth and tranquility of the house. Since there wasn't any point to feeling sorry for myself, I recalled a comforting email from a friend a few days earlier... We had been discussing the possibility of a fly-fishing visit to Pennsylvania over the weekend, if the heavy rains didn't blow-out the headwater streams. My friend is a married guy who has limited time to "play outdoors" on the weekend. He was working on a way to go fishing that Saturday while "trying to preserve domestic tranquility at home."

I answered one of his emails by saying, "I know what you mean about preserving that tranquility. It can be like walking a tightrope over a gorge." Moments later I read his response... "A really narrow rope... With the wind howling!"

"Amen," I answered, thankful that my own wife understands that fly-fishing and being in the wild helps to keep me stable, and domestically compatible. I wondered if my recent tumble into the bottomless creek was in some way like falling off a tightrope into a gorge... It couldn't be, I decided. There was peace at home. I had come back with all my bones intact. I felt clean—fresh, as if from an annual bath. The only similarity was in tipping over and getting soaked, experiencing a tight fit in any angler's passage through the understory.

5

Fly-fishing can be a greatly rewarding activity, and I certainly don't want to give the wrong impression by saying there's another side to all the fun involved. But let's face it: fishing can be work at times, no matter what society may think of recreational louts extolling the virtues of their craft.

There are no free lunches on this mortal coil, and I doubt that fly-fishers are granted any exceptions. Most of my fishing is a solitary business, so any loathsome utterances issued from my lips while on the water are likely to be heard only by the willow trees and warblers and are probably incapable of assaulting innocent ears. That said, I wonder if it's useful to present a list, my Top Five fly-fishing problems and vexations, as a kind of warning for anyone who might be in the neighborhood... Okay, here it is...

Problem #5—Leaky Waders. You'd think that a decent pair would last me for a couple of years at least before inviting the stream to come inside. I suppose, though, if you're rough on the equipment and you fish a hundred times a year, then a two-year life span on a pair of flashy "breathables" might not be so bad after all.

Problem #4—Timothy. I'm not sure of the genus and species of this tall streamside grass, but it's common through early summer and, damn it all, catches more than its share of back-cast flies and leader tippets for a meal. @&:*! Another one!

Problem #3—Trash. No need for description here. One hates to find it strung out on a willow branch or tossed out on a parking spot or at the edges of a favorite pool. It's almost as bad as vandalism in our parklands or graffiti found on natural artifacts. @*%# those idiots!

Problem #2—Yours Truly. Whether by impatience or ineptitude, I often get in the way of myself—which always threatens peace and clarity of mind. @#%* me! Stupid #&&#%$*!

And problem #1—Humanity-at-Large. When 4-wheelers cross and re-cross a favorite stream and erode the banks, when I find yet another empty beer can, or water bottle or disposable diaper hung up on a bush, I take it out on my own kind. As much as I love my friends and family and appreciate my readers and admire thousands of individuals on this planet, I admit there's just too many of us (how many billions now?) to sustain a healthy life on Earth.

What's a healthy number for humanity across the globe? I don't know, but maybe around the two-billion mark, a fourth of what we currently have. Sure, it's just a shot in the dark, a figure pulled out when considering people in balance with *all* the species of life around the world. I don't agree with the radical notion that to save our planet we should live long and healthy lives but stop reproducing. I don't agree with the suggestion that our species should work toward a peaceful but complete annihilation of itself. Extinction makes no sense to me, although it *would* solve a lot of problems that we face. We're a part of nature's grand design, and it's time we learn to deal with that by dealing with ourselves.

My suggestions then, for what they're worth… Go easy on the breeding business, and support adoption. Preserve more wilderness and help to educate each other. Who knows, people may eventually understand what we need to do to find real balance with the ultimate winner in the game of evolution. Sadly, it can't be said that history is on our side, despite all the social progress that we've made.

Other Top 10 fly-fishing vexations on my list of curses might include the following: weak blood-knots; wind knots; freezing temperatures; new leaders that won't unwind correctly from the packet; and failing eye-sight—a vicious problem that I hope doesn't rise much higher on my list.

If I had super-human powers I might know how to elevate myself, and all of us, above these curses on the stream and in the world. As it is, however, I'll keep wading onward through the waters of my understory, tumbling every now and then, for sure, but trying to appreciate the beauty wherever it is found.

Flycatcher

1

When the weather turned irresistible for the prospects of birding and casting a line for fish, I ventured to the West Branch Genesee and, later, to the main stem of the river. There, among the hills and hollows of the dual-state (NY and PA) watershed, I made my evening peace with the caddis fly. For three consecutive nights, I was ready for the caddis commonly known as the Grannom fly (*Brachycentrus americanus*), and the hatches were spectacular.

The West Branch is typically narrow, rocky and alder-lined, but the dark gray caddis was fluttering moth-like from the water, and the wild trout punched the surface with expectation. I was reeling in a miniature brook trout when I saw a large trout flash beneath it. Releasing the little fellow, I decided to try a Muddler Minnow as a lure for the predator. Before I could tie the Muddler on completely, though, I saw the big brown make a graceful leap from the water, almost nailing a Coffin Fly that sailed above the currents.

This was the kind of stuff that passionate anglers live for, though I don't know many who are willing to sacrifice their ease to fish the kind of brushy water that I found here. Truth be told, I'm often on it more by accident than by design. Anyway, I abandoned the Muddler Minnow for an imitation of a Coffin Fly and quickly had the brown trout on the line.

Each evening of the Grannom hatch, I was greeted by the *Vreep Vreep*! shrieking of the great-crested flycatcher. Other flycatchers, smaller species of *Empidonax* like the alder and the willow, called out with their quieter, weepy notes from nesting territories along the stream. These, and other songbirds, took their share of insects hatching from the water. A fly-fishing birdwatcher could go blissfully berserk in a place like this.

On the third night I was down below Genesee village on the main stem of the river in New York. The Grannom was hatching profusely by 6 p.m. and continued through the evening. The trout rose for the feed as if gravity became unhinged from the riverbed. I fished more leisurely now. The 9-foot rod, a 4-weight, stirred the air more slowly and rhythmically than the short rod when I worked it on the West Branch. Songbirds, trout and caddis flies were my company, their configuration changing minute by minute. The hatch would diminish, and the fishing would get slower for a while. The dark gray caddis would subside for the season and resettle in the depths. An egg and larval phase would temper in sub-aqueous earth. It might even be said that an angler's memory could stir from such a bedrock place.

2

If you inspect a naked bird, whether it be a nestling recently born or a chicken that's plucked and ready for the oven, you'll get an image of a creature that's evolved from the dinosaurs, a survivor of the asteroid impact and explosion, or of slower forms of volcanism, that signaled the end of the late Cretaceous Period. The naked bird, stripped of feathers, is a smoothed body, typically squat and tailless, with a set of spindly legs and skinny forelimbs. You might see that a bulging cranium sports big eyes and a prominent beak. It seems that birds are essentially small dinosaurs that developed into the more than ten-thousand species of feathered animal found throughout the world today.

From the near extinction of the dinosaurs, birds have evolved over the eons, diversifying from *Archaeopterix* (one of the archetypal birds that left feather fossils estimated to be 150 million-years-old) into the modern creatures with their wing bones and aerodynamic feathers. *Archaeopterix* was apparently raven-sized, with sharp teeth and jaws, but also had characteristics of today's great blue heron launching into flight. The scales on the legs and feet of a bird are a key to the connection between them and the reptiles. Ancestral birds like *Archaeopterix* developed slowly into new varieties of warm-blooded life with feathers.

Ornithologists believe that feathers evolved from reptilian scales that overlapped themselves and split, providing greater flexibility. Birds were becoming more mobile and more capable of escaping predation. The phenomenon of flight evolved into what most birds have today—an incredible perfection of aerodynamic power. Evolution continues; and the avian world continues to inspire the imagination of humans through art and science.

It's not surprising that our early historical records often link the flight of birds to the gods. Even the smallest of birds were viewed as being capable of flying past the constructs of humanity while transcending mortal concerns. Birds of prey were sometimes seen as powerful creatures with a god-like demeanor. Gods, angels and demons were personified with wings; birds occasionally had a sacred quality, preeminent in creation myths of early cultures.

The mythological phoenix came from China. This eagle-sized creature was the emperor of birds and symbolized the sun. The phoenix had a crest of feathers, sapphire eyes, and lived in a deathless paradise. However, when it reached the ripe old age of 500 years (or more), the bird descended to Earth, inspired to die and then immolate—to rise from its ashes with a vivid burst of energy to be reborn.

Birds have been important for our stories, legends and views on life. Icarus and his father Daedalus, creator of the Labyrinth on the ancient isle of Crete, designed a pair of wings with wax and feather so that Icarus might escape the island by flying like a bird. Daedalus warned his son not to fly too high or too low, risking a melt-down from the sun or the weight of dampness from the sea. Icarus flew and, giddy from flight and the hubris of his kind, forgot his father's sage advice. He flew too high and saw the wax melt from his feathers. He flapped his arms frantically but fell into the sea and drowned. We're left with a simple caveat— beware of what can happen if we take our dreams too seriously.

Owls are fascinating creatures of the night. Some early cultures believed that an owl's appearance, or its hooting in the dark, could be an omen of death. The North American Pawnees, on the other hand, considered the owl to be a shield against evil and darkness. Elsewhere, owls have been associated with such disparate subjects as black magic and founts of wisdom.

In the opening piece of my first published book of poetry, *Talking to the Owls* (1984), I wrote: "They awake in the imperfect/ Darkness of the swamps when/ Hawks return to roost, the great/ Eyes broadening to enclose the night. / Since the birth of rodents, flowering/ Plants, they have radiated toward / Our dreams, hunting various avenues/ For prey...."

All birds, in my estimation, radiate toward our dreams and challenge us to reply. One type of bird that currently challenges a reply from me is the flycatcher, the insect specialist, especially the group of flycatchers living in my area of the Northeast. These flycatchers include the eastern kingbird, the great-crested flycatcher, the eastern wood-pewee, the several smaller species of *Empidonax*, and the lovable eastern phoebe, the tail-wagger, that has built a nest on our porch every year that we've been living in this house.

Scientists have recognized that birds will often sample foods in a random manner, but experiments have also shown that insect consumers, like flycatchers, quickly learn to key in on edible favorites. They can focus on one insect species while rejecting other flying bugs—insects that may have a color or a pattern linked to unpleasant experiences. In other words, a flycatcher might hold an image of a satisfying morsel and continue to search for more of the same if it's available. A search for one species might continue if the "search image" in the flycatcher's brain says that the desired prey is on the wing. Thus, the feeding process is quick and easy and, if the theory is correct, learning and memory come into play.

I'm reminded of my own selection process when rummaging around for a certain artificial in the fly box. And with a small leap of imagination, one can think about the rising trout that refuses to leave an angler's memory—the fussy one, the trout so selective and wise about its feeding choices that it drives the fisherman to distraction or even to the brink of madness.

3

The work week was unwinding: I was standing at a check-out counter with a six of a favorite IPA, thinking of the fly-fishing prospects for the weekend (a constant struggle, keeping life's Big River in view) and a slew of odd jobs that required doing before an imminent trip out West.

A couple of young guys stood behind me in the line, waiting to pay for their own quantities of a popular "Lite." I tried to ignore their commentary on what must have been an attractive female in the store, but when I heard a fella say, "Old man knows good beer," I looked back at them and said, "Oh, you guys talking about *me*?"

"Yeah," said one guy, "I like your taste in beer." Now, I really don't mind being called old. I'm rather used to it. But I'm glad these whippersnappers weren't being facetious about my choice in brews. I checked myself to make sure my ears were on straight and that I hadn't heard, "Old man doesn't know *shit* about good beer."

I didn't have to raise my macho timber. I didn't have to make a fool of myself by saying, "Listen punk, if you wanna step outside, me and my IPA will kick your Lite Beer ass!" Instead we had a brief, sunny rap about alternatives and the choices that we make while forking over hard-earned dollars. After that, the world was just a little bit brighter.

As it was, the comment at the beer check-out made me feel more purposeful. Old age is seldom easy, but confidence is reassuring, especially when considering other more difficult choices that we make––those paths we've chosen to walk on into the future.

I'd taken a day from work to fish on Kettle Creek and to experience the Sulphur and Slate Drake hatches (not the strongest I've ever seen but satisfactory nonetheless). Then, I walked into the back country of a tributary where the brook trout were willing to take almost any dry fly pattern as long as my approach was quiet and respectful. I would also fish an upper stretch of Cross Fork Creek and find it pleasantly productive.

I was making progress in my preparation to see and fish great rivers in Colorado, Wyoming and Montana. Once again, I heard "Old man really knows good beer." I took it to mean more than simply a supermarket choice. If all goes well, I'll hit rivers like the South Platte and Frying Pan in Colorado. My wife and I will do some mountain hiking, maybe climb to a lake with cutthroat trout. If not now, when? The River of Life is calling. We'll move on to Wyoming's Snake, Greys and Gros Ventre rivers near the Tetons. We'll fish and hike in Yellowstone, then follow up on classic

Montana streams, and maybe find a few surprises. I felt keyed in like a flycatcher at a mayfly hatch.

I don't plan a strict itinerary. If an opportunity arises, I move toward my interest, based on experience and what may come of it. Financial and temporal limitations must be considered, of course. If I get the green light and my body says go, I'm set.

When my wife called me to dinner and I heaped the plate with fried catfish, seasoned crispy cauliflower and lemon-spiced arugula, I tasted everything with delight. The cold IPA, the Old Man's choice, was good accompaniment, but the dinner overall was surpassing.

It inspired me to take an evening hike up Dryden Hill to check on the fields with their bobolinks. I've always liked these interesting blackbirds and their bubbly song but, unfortunately, they were flying low and in the distance this year. Returning down the hill, collecting some trash along the way, I paused at a clearing and listened to a wood thrush piping, and a young red fox barking harshly from a ravine. A barred owl hooted from somewhere in the valley. Then I heard a different song…

I hadn't exactly given up on hearing whippoorwills in the East but, frankly, their numbers seem to be diminishing, and I hadn't heard or seen one in 38 years, since my days of living near the Blue Ridge Mountains. I had hopes of encountering them again, especially since a friend had played a recording of one while we were fishing Slate Run a couple of years before. He had captured the call notes of a whippoorwill encountered near his home in northern Pennsylvania. And now I was hearing one again.

Whip-poor-will, whip-poor-will..., on and on. I listened and followed as the bird moved slowly down the valley toward my home. Eventually the bird flew over the creek and started up the other hillside with its lush green forest. I imagined the bird's wide gaping mouth sweeping up erratic moths and other flying insects as it winged its way with ceaseless energy. It seemed to rise above the small clearings, perhaps looking for a mate to settle with for a season, fading slowly from my auditory range as it flew on into the long river of the night.

Desert Rainbows

Is there not much in nature and in life that is symbolized by the rainbow? Nature is not all solids and fluids and gases; the unreal, the fantastic, the illusory play a large part in our lives.

– John Burroughs

1

The night rain of New Mexico spreads across the sand and binds the billions of particles for a light impression of foot and claw. The kit fox emerges, and the jack rabbit, and the great horned owl. The darkling beetle wakes with the dawn. The sun calls a black-throated sparrow into song. The bleached lizard runs from an approaching foot that makes an imprint on the sand.

Leaves of cottonwood track the surface of the ground from a wind-tossed limb. The primrose petals radiate; the jack rabbit and coyote run. Water binds the gypsum desert of White Sands National Monument (recently re-designated as a national park) only inches from the surface.

White Sands encompasses 275 square smiles of desert. The Sands form an oasis in a chalk dry Chihuahua Desert bowl. Sure, it's a long way to the

trout streams that I love to haunt, but wait a minute...
As water binds the particles of gypsum, it urges every
dune crest into motion, blowing on the wind toward the
places we know and love. And as a wilderness moves,
the white dunes invite: movies have been filmed here;
Pink Floyd played a concert on the 90's sand. I try to
imagine night-walking on the dunes with a full moon
overhead, the starkness and the hazard now soft and
beautiful... Could I find a *rivertop* in such a vast and
waterless realm? That's crazy! Then again, "There's
water at the bottom of the ocean," as the Talking Heads
declared in song. So maybe there's a river, a trout
stream even, flowing through adjacent sands.

2

Even with climate change and the problem of
expanding desert in various locations around the globe,
I found a good trout stream within an hour's drive of
Alamogordo, New Mexico and the White Sands
National Park by driving eastward into the Sacramento
Mountains and their Lincoln National Forest. I began to
fish the Rio Penasco for its rainbow trout while
ruminating sadly that its native fish, the Rio Grande
cutthroat, can no longer be found within its high-desert
confines.

Native trout in much of the semi-arid West are
particularly imperiled by the prospect of a warming
climate and desertification. Many of its populations
have become unstable and diminished by the
introduction of non-native rainbow trout which all too
readily interbreed with cutthroat throat, producing
hybrid fish incapable of reproduction.

Feeling the urge to fly-fish while visiting and traveling through the Southwest, I thought of cold-water species native to the semi-arid lands—the Apache, Gila, and golden trout, as well as the Colorado River and Rio Grande sub-species of cutthroat—but settled happily with the stocked and wild fish of the Rio Penasco.

3

Halfway between the sweltering Tularosa Basin and the cool pine forests of the Lincoln National Forest in southern New Mexico, we stopped to view the canyon where Archaic Peoples ostensibly took shelter in their travel thousands of years ago.

Since I like to know the landforms and some basic natural history of new localities that I'm entering, I instinctively raise antennae to get a sense of my surroundings. Preparing for a fly-fishing excursion to the Rio Penasco beyond Cloudcroft (the highest town in New Mexico), I gladly tagged along with my wife and brother-in-law as we escaped the desert's summer heat with a short drive into the forest.

At Cloudcroft, nearly 9000 feet above sea-level, a walk felt as good as an August swim. An insipid shopping stroll was bearable, and a good seat at the neighborhood saloon for a burger and beer was even better.

We took a scenic drive along the mountain rim toward Sunspot. There the westward views across the basin and of White Sands were exhilarating. Trailheads beckoned. We did a walking tour of Sunspot with its National Solar Observatory overlooking the Missile

Range in the Tularosa Basin. The dry, clean air, plus abundant sunshine, makes this place an ideal location for scientific studies of the sun.

I found the birds to be amazing: bands of western bluebirds roamed the pine-scented meadows; mountain chickadees and black-throated gray warblers fed among the shrubbery. I added Grace's warbler to my life-list of birds encountered. But what did all this have to do with fly-fishing?

We made a right turn onto the Upper Rio Penasco Road. I'd never been there before but figured we were near the headwaters of the stream I would soon be fishing. A recent storm had flooded the river and dashed an opportunity to explore it earlier, but here at the springs the sudden appearance of flowing water was exciting.

A rivulet spilled into the meadow. I left the car and crossed a short bit of national forest ground. Surprisingly, the rivulet tumbled into a deep clear pool. Cold water, several feet deep, was a pleasant introduction to a river I'd never inspected before.

That night, a monsoon thunderstorm rattled the basin in Alamogordo but left it with little rain (much less than the mountaintops had received). I thought of the headwaters pool and felt comforted. The depth there, the tranquility of water in elk country seemed like a third eye in a meditative trance. I saw the long river below, and an eastern guy ready to fish it.

4

New Mexico has a world-class trout fishery in the San Juan River, but it also has a few mountain and desert streams of rare quality. One of the lesser known spring creeks flows through the high ground of the southern sector and is fished by various angling notables, many of whom report that gaining access to it is well worth the effort.

The Rio Penasco is a 40-mile spring creek in the Sacramento Mountains and the Pecos River watershed, one of the finest trout streams in desert country. Its headwaters lie in the Lincoln National Forest near Cloudcroft, New Mexico. The fishing starts to get interesting downstream of Mayville, along U.S. 82, but most of the good opportunities are on private ranches where the river is leased by angling clubs. In the past, while visiting family in Alamogordo, I'd been deterred from traveling to the river because of the expense, but then I found a way of fishing and enjoying the Penasco at a modest cost.

I became a member of Mesilla Valley Fly Fishers (MVFF), a conservation-minded group of anglers based in Las Cruces, NM, that has a two-mile lease of the Penasco at the Runyon Ranch. For a reasonable purchase of a daily permit from the MVFF, you can fly-fish for stocked and wild trout. The club stocks German browns and small rainbows that can grow quickly in the nutrient-rich waters. The rainbows reproduce in various sections of the stream and can grow to healthy sizes, a few of them obtaining lengths of 20 inches or more.

When Chuck Mueller, then the president of MVFF, volunteered to drive up from Las Cruces to meet me in Alamogordo and then to introduce me to the river, I jumped at the opportunity. We drove up to the ranch and began to fish where the regulations are strictly catch-and-release, with the use of barbless hooks only.

The stream was flowing a little high and muddy from recent "monsoon" thunderstorms, but it was fishable. The only morning flies we noted were some Blue-winged Olive spinners, but no rise forms were detected. I worked downstream casting a variety of imitations including Grasshopper and foam Beetle, but nothing was working. Rejoining Chuck at lunch time, I learned that he was having some success with streamers.

After sandwiches (with plenty of water because the dry heat can drain you in no time), Chuck insisted that I fish with him upstream. I would cut my leader to about a 3x diameter and tie on a big old pattern like the Olive Sculpin. We would fish the afternoon with streamers.

We didn't catch many trout before the typical mountain thunderstorm rolled in around 3 p.m., but the one I did catch made the effort worthwhile. Returning to the city, I was thankful for the river guidance and vowed to stay in touch with MVFF people who involve themselves with conservation projects, not to mention all the fishing trips that members plan together. I was ready to return next day for a solo excursion on the river.

Back on the Penasco, I found that the water had risen a little from the latest storm, but the fishing was improved. I covered old ground and waded into the new. It felt good to fish in desert solitude, in the dry mountain air, but occasionally the freshness of the river was unnerving. Greenhorn that I was, I had come prepared for wet wading but, instead of arriving with neoprene wading socks and shoes (as Chuck had worn), I fished in shorts and sandals totally inadequate when sinking almost knee-deep into silt, or when traversing steep banks while keeping an eye out for rattlesnakes.

The Rio Penasco is frequently a clear spring creek that requires the use of long fine leaders when fly-fishing but, in two days of casting on the water, it was relatively high and off-colored. There are numerous deep holes in the river, and the trick was to get the fly down quickly. Unlike many eastern spring creeks, the Penasco didn't have the bane of vegetation that tangles with a back-cast fly.

Although dry flies weren't producing, weighted nymphs and streamers (Prince and Copper John and Sculpin) were the ticket. I caught more rainbow trout, heavy fish, than I expected, and looked forward to the possibility of another visit someday. The high desert country has an undefinable allure, and when its waters call, I find it difficult to ignore.

5

For all the damage that non-native trout may or may not inflict on native populations in the West, I've come to appreciate the browns and rainbows in such places as the Rio Penasco. I would prefer the native cutthroat that once inhabited the river, but that's not the reality today. We can work toward restoration of native trout where such labor is appropriate, but for now I'll take the fishing where I can find it.

I like the image of a desert rainbow in a largely rainless place. Symbolically, the rainbow brings a promise that our troubles will end, if only for a day or two. It's as if I can see a wild trout with a red shimmer in an arch above a watery horizon. Even if the only downpour that had recently occurred was that of *sand*, the consequent image of a rainbow is a pleasant picture.

Desert rainbows, like the rainbow trout in a beautiful stream, can bring suggestions of peace and new beginnings. A religious person might suggest that a sign has been given from above—that the Earth shall not be destroyed, at least not today. I'll accept the image of the rainbow as a stroke of luck, a figurative pot of gold at the end of another fishing excursion.

As I delve into my theme of life portrayed as a sinuous, non-linear river of dreams, I also think of practical matters. I can say that the Penasco is reputed to have excellent fly hatches through the season. Mayflies, caddis and terrestrials will be found. The wild browns and rainbow trout are less selective in their feeding habits than on many spring creeks in the country, thanks to the remoteness of the stream and to the bounty of its mostly excellent weather that allows some hatches to have greater duration than in other locales. For example, the tiny Trico mayfly can appear on the river from March through November.

Blue-winged Olives, Elk-hair Caddis and nymphs such as Hare's-Ear, Prince, and Zug Bug in sizes 12-18 are effective. Leggy grasshopper patterns can be deadly from summer on through fall. Midges, scuds, damselflies, and streamer patterns can fill out your list for desert-country trout. My one covenant of delight is to say, the fish will be there.

Top of the Rockies

1

While staying at a family base near Colorado Springs I had done some fishing on the South Platte River, and now it was time to reinspect the Rockies. The fine summer redolence of cool mountain air began to stir the human spirit, as birdsong and wildflower drifted through our senses. For an easterner, each entry into these mountains can seem as fresh and exciting as a first experience of the West.

I was gathering details of a new place: remembering an observation of a cut-bow trout in the net, the sighting of a soaring Swainson's hawk, the view of an American dipper flying short-winged over river rocks, the glimpse of scarlet gilia from the window of a speeding car... Adding details for a fresh sense of place, enlarging one share of the human experience, like building an attractive new room at the house of life.

We drove from Buena Vista and a rest stop at a beer and pizza terrace, climbing past a Rocky Mountain pinnacle at Mt. Elbert, then paused for a tundra walk along the flower-spangled, snowy patches of Independence Pass. The wildflowers and breath-taking scenery at 12,000 feet above sea-level set a tone of expectation and excitement for the road ahead.

I remembered reading of Enos Mills (1870-1922), a Colorado mountain writer and guide whose work helped to establish Rocky Mountain National Park in a northern sector of the state. Mills was a latter-day frontiersman who valued self-reliance and rugged individualism, combining these quintessential American traits with the sensitivity of a modern nature guide. He felt that a naturalist could guide inquisitive souls to the secrets of nature and the numberless points of fascination contained by many plants and animals, as well as to the stories hidden behind each stream and stone—at least in theory. He strove to reveal the wonders of the Colorado wilderness and the poetry of nature at its heart. Our high passage toward Aspen and beyond provided us a partial understanding of the naturalist's pursuit.

I had plans to fish the famous Frying Pan River near Basalt. We took a campsite at Ruedi Reservoir which, for me, was most notable for a western fox sparrow singing sweetly in the shrubs nearby. The evening Frying Pan, a tail-water fishery in a red-stone canyon, had a very cool 45-degree (F.) temperature, but the wild browns were rising to a Black Ant drifted on the pools and riffles, as well as to mayfly spinners settling from their flights above.

Rather than fishing the renowned "Toilet Bowl," the big plunge-pool at the foot of Ruedi Dam, the site for oversized rainbows fattened on Mysis shrimp, I opted for lonelier water downstream from the knot of fishermen. The red-stone walls and the brown trout suited me fine in that location. My choice of place for casting dry flies didn't make me a better angler, but I probably enjoyed the outing more.

Next day, we moved on to a national forest campground 17 miles from a town along the Eagle River. I had camped there (at 9000 feet) with family members 22 years before. The mountain serenity, the aspens, the blue columbines, and the fly-fishing had made a deep impression on me. Now the campground seemed larger than before, but the beauty remained intact. Fools Peak, a mountain I had climbed (and written of in my book *Sand & Sage*, 2010), lorded over the valley from its upstream vantage on eternity.

Here the trout stream has a gravel bed, with deep undercut pools and riffles. Fishing for its wild brook and brown trout is delightful. Sadly, the native cutthroat is gone from all but the headwater near Fools Peak. The trout near our camp, and along the three miles of a loop trail through the meadows and forest, rose handily to my dry fly offerings, especially to a Royal Wulff and a Rusty Spinner.

On our last morning in camp, we dressed hastily in bone-chilling cold. Frost covered the blooms and vegetation along the creek as we began one final hike at this location and waited for the sun to rise and bathe the valley in light. We felt more comfortable inside the forest. The tranquility of land and water was highlighted by birds—pine grosbeaks, white-crowned sparrows and Swainson's thrushes—and by firs and spruces sweeping upward toward the peaks.

Traveling westward toward Wyoming, I recalled an earlier summer in Colorado when we were joined by my son and his wife for a visit to Rocky Mountain National Park. On that occasion I had fished for greenback cutthroats in a stream where I had caught them on a previous visit. This time all I found there was the eastern native, the brook trout, and I learned later that a destructive flood occurring in the intervening years had pushed out or destroyed the iconic cutthroat from that area of idyllic streams. I reconnected with the greenback, eventually, by means of a backcountry hike to the lakes. As for the Fall River and its tributaries where the damaging flood occurred, the presence of water ouzels, the American dipper, promised that the cutthroats would regain the valley once again. Even if these tail-bobbing, streambed-walking, gray birds shouldn't be personified, I found that they had to be believed.

In the tundra region of the park that summer, I added two more species to my life-list of birds—the rosy finch and white-tailed ptarmigan (which surprised me by its songbird size). From there we traveled west and north along the wind-driven heights, and I swore that I could see Wyoming out across the Colorado River headwaters and the Never Summer Mountains.

Most recently, arriving in Alpine, Wyoming, my wife and I joked about retirement in this community if we could afford its balanced charm—its small size, its hub of three fine rivers, with fly shops, comfortable motel, saloons, and crazy red-white-and blue restaurant, not to mention its great mountain scenery. For about a year (since our previous visit), I'd been dreaming to fish the Greys River nearby. I was glad to find that the Greys River Road, which had been closed because of a winter landslide, was reopened and ready for exploration.

Due to winter run-off, the Greys was flowing high at 1350 cubic feet per second and certainly wasn't wade-able, but it didn't take long for me to achieve my goal of catching and releasing the beautiful and gutsy Snake River fine-spotted cutthroat. The Greys River flows for 50 miles or more through the Bridger National Forest. My initial cutthroats were small and came from a feeder stream. Then I hooked and landed the first of several large fine-spotted trout by casting a conehead Muddler Minnow through the heavier water of the Greys.

Every landscape here and in neighboring Grand Tetons National Park seemed buoyant in the fresh weather of early July. A couple of western tanagers flew above the riverbanks and added their own brand of color to the place. Gentians, gilia and lupines starred the meadows near the mountain roads. The Snake River, the very life-blood of the magnificent Tetons, captured our imaginations, too.

A pair of bald eagles chased an osprey, trout in talons, over the river and eventually forced the smaller bird to drop the fish. The trout was snapped up in mid-air by a feathered interloper. Down below this action, a family of river otters cavorted in the grasses and did not seem overly concerned about a party of kayakers passing by.

We enjoyed a walk to Leigh Lake beneath the splendid peaks of Moran and Grand Teton and, if that wasn't enough, our next morning ride to Yellowstone National Park brought a first sighting of a timber wolf. The large canine had raced across the highway and then paused a short distance away to allow a glimpse of its eyes and its healthy coat of hair, the color of which reminded me of hackle in an Adams dry fly. The following day, well inside the park, we saw a second timber wolf—a black female that I photographed as she headed homeward along the cold, full-flowing Lamar. Grizzly bears were evident, as well. Our best sighting of these cinnamon-colored beasts occurred on a roadway near the Gibbon River.

Bison, of course, were abundant in the park. I was catching rainbow trout while standing in the Firehole when a big bull bison lumbered onto the highway and brought the car and RV traffic to a standstill. The indifferent fellow shuffled along the pavement at a summer pace. The vehicle drivers, anxious for Old Faithful's scheduled eruption, had to wait. A few impatient drivers tried to slip past the animal, but he figuratively flipped them off by shaking his massive head while stomping into their path.

Meanwhile, my wife sat with her novel in a lawn chair planted by the Firehole River and chuckled at the powers of a solitary bison nearby. I felt entertained, myself, resuming to cast for trout rising to the latest hatch in the sulfur-tainted flow.

3

Like many hardcore anglers I love to fish Montana streams and rivers. The Big Hole with its bonus touch of grayling; the Madison for its hatches and big trout;

the Gallatin for its rainbows and mountain scenery; the Bitterroot branches for their cutthroat trout and Ponderosa pines; Rock Creek for its splendid isolation—all of it, and more, enough for several lifetimes of exploration. On this occasion, my wife and I were headed for a new adventure in Glacier National Park.

In 1915, Dr. Lyman Sperry, an engineer and mountain explorer, wrote to the Kalispell Chamber of Commerce and *The Kalispell Bee* saying, "A national park highway should have not only fine natural scenery, but exhibitions of ingenious skill. It should have at least a few tunnels, galleries, terraces, bridges, hairpin turns, and all that sort of thing—to produce the surprises, thrills and joys that tourists seek." The proposed highway for Glacier National Park, the so-called Going-to-the-Sun road, would be all what Dr. Sperry dreamed it could be, and more.

I've never been a major fan of roadways, no matter their construction, but I'll admit that the 50-mile highway climbing through Glacier National Park must be seen to be believed. If you're unwilling or unable to experience the wild beauty of the park's interior, then the road can take you into a jaw-dropping and mind-blowing realm. In a recent book about Glacier, author C. W. Guthrie writes: "That this road exists and somehow seems to belong is a marvel of engineering and gritty determination to do it right." *Going-to-the-Sun Road* (2006) portrays a fascinating natural history of the park as well as an intriguing account of how this road was planned and eventually constructed.

The 20-year construction of this singular highway in Glacier National was designed to stand "supreme and alone," and that it does, blending in admirably with rushing streams, lakes and towering alpine mountains. We who drove it several times, in the company of all too many other summer tourists, reveled in the wonders of this place and sadly said farewell to the remnant glaciers now receding into the indifferent arms of climate change.

It's been said that Glacier National Park (adjoined with Waterton Lakes National Park in Alberta, Canada) contains the most stunning scenery in America, and I am not prepared to argue such opinion. Glacier's narrow highway was the first in any national park constructed to complement and harmonize with the natural surroundings while minimizing damage to the neighboring environment. When first designed, the road's construction was considered, by some, to be impossible. But as we traveled its seamless and tortured miles, the only time the road did not feel artfully constructed was when the traffic choked because a driver saw a bear or mountain goat and couldn't reach a pull-over spot. At that point, you might be hanging over a thousand-foot drop-off while staring at the face of Bird Woman Falls or Heaven's Peak and wondering who was crazier—the original designers or yourself for wanting to drive up here. It's no place to be if the Earth suddenly quakes.

The architectural features of the route from West Glacier to St. Mary, Montana are too numerous to detail, but a traveler can't ignore the road's 22-foot width that narrows significantly along 10 miles of the "Garden Wall." Additionally, there are memorable moments to be found along the six percent road-grade from "The Loop" to Logan Pass. You'll drive through two tunnels and traverse eight bridges. You may note the road culverts for the numerous streams. The 40,000 feet of native-stone guard walls at the mountainsides can be appreciated (especially near the Triple Arches at the Garden Wall). Each year, the upkeep of the highway is a monumental affair. The snow and rock removal, alone, can stagger the imagination.

But we didn't come here just to marvel at a manmade wonder. We came for an honest look at the "crown of the continent," this place of rivertops where, in theory, we might see its waters flowing to the far Pacific, Gulf of Mexico and Hudson Bay. What began with musings on the Western streams and mountains from my Dryden Hill summit, months before, continued with our visions here at Glacier. We were only scratching the surface, certainly, but it was pleasant to contemplate this 16,000 square-mile wonderland containing parts of two mountain ranges and over 130 named lakes. We were high up and exposed to the mysterious forces of the world beyond our skins. The linear routes of nature, the trails I once explored or dreamed of exploring, took on the dimensions of the sky and universal canopy. Words get lost here; languages dissolve in the wind and mountain clarity.

We had pitched our tent at Apgar Campground near the crystalline waters of Lake McDonald following a night spent at Tully Lake, about 25 miles from Whitefish. The wild environment at Tully is one of the few Montana locations where the common loon is found to be nesting. We were lucky to get our Apgar site at Glacier National by arriving early on a Monday morning.

Although Glacier is a hiking and a backcountry paradise, we found that a designated campground was the best bet for the limited amount of time we had available. From there, our short hikes and fishing forays would insure some insight into the park.

Most of the streams and rivers in the park are glacially fed and thus too clear and sterile, lacking in nutrients for good trout fishing, but they certainly looked attractive to a die-hard fisherman like myself. McDonald Creek seemed incredibly clear and cold, its water flowing over gem-like stones and gravel. It didn't matter that its insect life was almost nonexistent, and that its trout seemed few and far between. It just felt extraordinary to stand by its presence and to cast beneath the awesome peaks of Glacier.

Avalanche Creek was a different story. My wife and I strolled the mile-long boardwalk, a circuit trail, along this tributary of McDonald Creek, and wound through an imposing stand of western cedar and black poplar trees. Although grizzly bears are a major presence in the park, we felt confident that the bears in the vicinity were well fed on their usual prey and wouldn't be a worry. I was carrying a small bamboo fly rod for some wet-wading in the area. After catching and releasing countless native trout, small cutthroats up to 10 inches long, I decided that the fish population here was stabilized, despite having a meager diet.

To round out our discoveries in northwestern Montana, we left Glacier Park occasionally for a quick visit to a brewery or a family-style restaurant. These forays were punctuated by stops at fishing holes along the South Branch and (especially) the Middle Fork Flathead River where I could make a long cast and successfully land a few west-slope cutthroats. We could leave the park and then reenter it at will, secure in the knowledge that the mountains held us like a home.

Rockpiles & Columbines

1

A black stonefly came to rest on the pinnacle of a rock cairn built beside a trout stream. The insect perched immobile on a small round stone that seemed to have an outlook on the field of rocks strewn widely along the stream. Ten or 12 feet from the rock cairn stood a singular plant, a lovely orange columbine hanging its bell-like blossom on the late spring microcosm I had entered.

The rockpile and the columbine, along with the vision of a stonefly in the sunlight, reduced my stress and provided some comfort. It was a typically hectic time of year for me. In addition to the usual jobs demanding attention, I needed to tie flies for my next few outings on the stream. Somehow, after whipping up a batch of nymph and dry fly patterns, I lost all the flies before including them in my boxes. I'd been moving in one direction and the world had been turning the opposite way. The flies had been scattered who knows where—to the dust bunnies, cats, or ravenous vacuum cleaner. The balance of a rock cairn juxtaposed with a flowering columbine was lost. I felt less organized than a stonefly resting on the pile.

Here, in late May and early June, there's a green explosion of new life outdoors. To see and to experience it, I needed to set priorities and step forward slowly and deliberately with balance. I needed to consider the contrary forces and opposing energies of life and meet their resolution calmly, if possible. Maybe I needed to become revolutionary and do something drastic. Maybe I needed to mow my lawn *before* I went fishing—even if it went against the grain of my desires.

Most of us can afford to slow down the hectic pace of life when things get stressful, even if the only strategy available is to take a deep breath in an easy chair. We can breathe more slowly, rhythmically, like the stonefly resting on the cairn. Personally, I'll try to make the most of what I see; I'll take a deeper inhalation of the dying lilac blossoms, try to peer down through the flowering columbine's comb and do whatever it takes to slow the rapid passage of time.

As the poet William Blake once noted, the contrary forces of life, the competing tendencies within us (good vs. evil, love vs. hate, etc.) can drive us mad if we're not careful. Christianity might claim that the contraries stem from an original sin committed in the Garden of Eden. Sinners might redeem themselves from evil by following a creed, but Blake believed that the restoration of a wayward soul could be achieved through trial and *vision*. Finding one's identity, the human center where happiness and satisfaction dwell, could be attained through creativity—the work of art and personal vision.

I don't want to oversimplify this Blakean vision or pretend to understand it completely, but I think the poet meant that vision is important in our lives; it's a rare commodity because of our inherent inclination to be rational creatures bent on pure materialism. We create a wall around the limited life we lead, a wall precluding vision and the full opening of our senses. We get wrapped up in our *busy-ness*; our trout flies blow off in the wind occasionally; our stone cairns wash out with the rising water, and the columbines deflower in the wild unseen.

2

Columbines are a personal favorite among the wildflowers. The spurred petals of this flower are unique. The spur formations can be found within the Set of Fives: the five sepals, five petals, and five pistils. Columbine must have said to its Creator: "Give me Five! I'll have nectar down inside my tubes. I'll feed the long-beaked moths and hummingbirds!"

The columbine has an indisputable connection to the birds. The flower's common name is derived from the Latin word for "dove" because the image of a columbine inverted seemed to mirror five doves in a cluster. The columbine belongs to the genus *Aquilegia*, a name derived from the Latin word for "eagle" since the flower was believed to resemble an eagle's claw. Imagining a mountain breeze stirring a colony of columbine flowers is like watching the blossoms lift their wings to fly!

Columbines, or *rockbells* (as I like to call them), are perennials of the garden or the wilderness. Here, at home, numerous hybrids do quite well domestically, and a wilder species thrives in semi-shaded, well-drained soil of rocky hills and river country. The eastern red columbine (*Aquilegia canadensis*) is the orange and yellow beauty that I like to inspect as much as possible but, for me, the most stunning blossom in my rockbell folder is the blue Colorado columbine (*A. alpina*) dwelling in or near the aspen groves of western mountains. Yellow columbine (*A. flavescens*) is a species that I've found more recently, an attractive flower native to the high meadows and Rocky Mountain slopes. Together, these species of columbine, as well as those I've yet to locate, form a spiritual component in my stony life with poetry.

As for rockpiles, I have no interest in pursuing the ancient art of stacking irregular stones. What has happened in the aftermath of the "Harmonic Convergence" events of the late 1980s is beyond me, but I know that cairns are striking features in the world of outdoor travelers. Cairns have long been used for a variety of purposes—as landmarks, monuments, directional markers—but they seem to become pointless or even subversive when constructed by those with too much time on their hands. When stones are stacked indiscriminately, they can be confusing to a hiker or even be construed as a disturbance to the local environment. Stones, removed from their natural placement, expose the soil once beneath them and endanger the homes of tiny creatures there. The soil gets washed away, eroded by the next hard rain.

Still, the modern cairn can be a beautiful structure, a landmark that connects a visitor to one who came before. Although I prefer my rockpiles left by natural process rather than by artful balancers in a meditative trance, I like to reflect on the small cairn by the trout stream and know that a kindred spirit had been there before me. Although the rockpile wasn't built with a leave-no-trace philosophy, I like the fact that a stonefly found it useful to be resting on the top, and that a lovely columbine grew nearby.

3

The Zen Buddhist term *satori* means insight or enlightenment. I know it's dangerous to apply the term to fly-fishing experiences because, as nearly everyone might suspect, fishing is a recreational activity and usually not considered a spiritual undertaking. Leave it to a local fishery to put me straight and to throw out categorical statements.

Rock Creek gave me an insight recently. I'm not referring to the famous trout stream in Montana or to Rock Run in northern Pennsylvania which writers like Charles Meck have referred to as "the most breathtaking picturesque trout stream in the Keystone State." I'm referring to a small stream only minutes from where I live. I fished it once, about 30 years ago, and then ignored it until recently.

An inexplicable power pulled me back to this small stream that tumbles from a forested divide. The stream planted me squarely in its series of waterfalls and plunge-pools lively with native trout. So where had I been all these years? In short, I was fishing brooks and rivers far and wide, effectively ignoring my back yard, as if Rock Creek had been less worthy of my efforts, a mere shadow of its former glory as a wild stream in the upper Susquehannock watershed. I'd built a wall around myself, around the small stream's possibilities, around its brook trout and spring wildflowers, so I had to set things straight.

I don't know where the Zen-like insight came from, where the rap to the head was delivered, unless it came from the creek itself. If we're lucky, we realize that, no matter our age, we're a student of life until we're dead. We have mentors that include the streams and forests, the oceans and deserts, the mountains and stars. We're always ready for that whack to the head, the sudden realization that we're a part of something larger than we know. When the contrary forces of the mind align themselves in resolution, a light comes on, the rockpile and columbine are in balance. When I thought of Blake's vision in the context of this stream, a new understanding seemed to flower.

My decades of fly-fishing experience have seldom offered me the luxury of insight. More typically I've been focused on the next rise or the next strike. I've been watching a butterfly or a bird or wondering childlike what I'll find around the next bend in the stream. I've been overly concerned, perhaps, about where my next beer or meal is coming from. A new insight is a flowering within, a luxury compared to all of that, more akin to working at a desk than to casting on a stream or lake. But when it comes, I'll take it— happy that a place like Rock Creek made an offer.

4

Whenever I start to think I'm spending too much time on the road or on the river, I remind myself that, in comparison, more time is spent on my back 40, on my small acreage with its paths behind the house. I call them "paths to nowhere," and I like the homebound feeling they provide that has no compass for what lies beyond. I'll walk the paths occasionally when I feel like doing absolutely nothing other than allowing my view to be encompassed by a pensive, meditative mood, with nowhere to go but here.

On those occasions, a ramble will take no account of work, school, or shopping mall. There's no fishing here, no hunting, buying, or warring with the elements. I might listen to the barred owl's eight-note calling, to the blue jay's squawking, and the catbird's mew. I'll check out the latest blossoms to appear— today it's the goldenrod, the aster and the turtlehead. I'll walk the paths through blackberry vines, poplar trees, autumn olives, and hundreds of Norway spruce, red pine, and apple trees. I won't go anywhere, really.

I'll stop to contemplate the gravesite of our old dog, Brook, and peer upward at the aging barn. That building has seen the happier days of agriculture, before my time, and the years of land abuse that I can only speculate about. A part of this place is growing wild; a part of it has been an anchor hold that slows my drifting on the sea of time. All of it, together, seems appropriate for me and who I am, a singular being in the outward change.

One hot day in July I was looking at a blank page in my journal book and wondering what to write. Since I've been writing journal entries for more than four decades now, I usually know what to do, but not always. When in doubt, I can always think about the writing process and continue the path to understanding. If I open my senses, I'll discover something new. A naturalist finds a trail mark ahead and has an opportunity to scratch some notes about it in a journal. I am careful about calling myself a naturalist. The writer John Hay once said that a true naturalist attains "high standards of knowledge and effort," and that sets the bar pretty high for me. As an amateur, though, I have flexibility and can set the bar wherever I want it.

I hadn't seen the prairie warbler in years. Maybe I could take this early morning opportunity to find the bird in its typical habitat of uphill shrubbery before the air became too hot and humid. It was time to hike with my binoculars.

I found heavy rocks flipped upside-down near the back line of my property. The flat rocks had roofed a world of ants inside the soil. The ground, torn in several locations, told the tale of bear. I kept my eyes open for the chance of seeing He-Who-Flips-the-Rocks, the stone turner who has no need for artful cairns, although my chances for encountering Mr. Bear seemed less probable than witnessing Lady Godiva riding bareback over the hill.

My writing process starts with what I know and what lies close at hand. I would note my climb through the tall grass of the steep hill, with my walking stick pushing aside the young growth of summer. I would listen for distinctive call notes of a prairie warbler, for the rising, high-pitched *zi-zI-ZI!* delivered against the humid air. I would listen, too, for the yellowthroat, song sparrow, field sparrow, mourning dove, and cedar waxwing, trying to remember what I heard in case I needed context for the writing of my words.

I didn't hear the white-and-yellow songster, the prairie warbler, until I had descended from the high ground and come to a stop. I'd been watching and listening to a willow flycatcher in the autumn-olive shrubbery when I finally saw it—a fleeting life that seemed to check me out while darting from bush to bush. And that's the thing about the prairie warbler and so many other creatures of a rural landscape. If you don't stop to watch and listen, if you're just passing by in thought that there is little more to see, you'll miss it.

Blending in with your environment makes all the difference when you're out. Any good hunter will tell you that. So, I pause, listen and take stock. I'll have something for the journal page, like an artist who feels the spirit of a place coming through to make a difference in how a landscape is perceived. A *balancer of stones* might take a childlike step and make a small adjustment to his or her relationship with nature. With a little work, almost anyone can be centered modestly between the inner self and the wildlife just beyond.

5

The western landscapes of America form a country so large and so indifferent to our whims and fascinations that, together, they seem almost mythical. Even in this day and age, the myth of the American West can grip imagination. The land has space, unpeopled space, and much of it is wild. Civilization has spread a thin veneer across those wilder places but, as the nature writer Mary Austin once remarked, those places are a strange mix of "God, death, beauty and madness." Landscape is a primary character in the work of many Western writers and artists, sacred locales still figure in the lives of Native Americans; and weather is important to nearly everyone sketching out a life in this sector of the nation.

My wife and I traveled eastward through Wyoming, drawn by the geography and myths of the land, while fortified by recent sightings of birds and wildflowers, e.g., the blue and yellow columbines of the higher mountain regions. Our new destination was Devils Tower National Monument near the South Dakota Badlands.

Devils Tower rises dramatically from the prairie and the Belle Fourche River in an area known as the Bear Lodge Mountains of Wyoming. The Tower is an igneous butte that stands 867 vertical feet from base to summit. A sacred site to many Native Americans in the region, the Tower is comprised of fluted columns of stone with hundreds of parallel cracks from top to bottom. Climbers are drawn to the Tower from around the world.

In 1906, Devils Tower became the first national monument in America when President Theodore Roosevelt officially recognized its significance. Long before that, the great formation played a part in the sacred rites of indigenous people such as the Kiowa and Lakota Sioux. Native American ceremonies continue there today, especially during the month of June.

The Tower, an eroded mass of igneous rock, or *laccolith*, had uplifted from earth some 60 million years ago as magma rose through layers of sedimentary stone, eventually wearing out to what we see today—a huge gray-green butte ablaze with white feldspar crystals in the early morning sun.

Roughly 40 million years ago, the magma cooled enough to contract and form the six-foot-wide hexagonal columns that, in a cross-section view, appear to have cracks formed at 120-degree angles. As we walked around Devils Tower on the 1.3-mile trail developed by the Park Service, and as we poked in and out of scree (the piles of rock column broken into stone and boulder), we were awestruck by Earth's tremendous powers.

As a fly-fisher I could look up at the vertical rise of six-sided stone and be reminded of a tapered bamboo fishing rod, hexagonal and exquisite in design. As a birder, I could peer at the upper heights and summit of the rock and see not the eagle or the doves associated with scientific and common names of columbine, but the actual flights of nesting peregrine falcons (and watchful prairie falcons) that feed on the numerous rock doves and other prey near the Tower. And as tourists, we might have been reminded of the Indian legends that connect the origins of the place, one of which could be encapsulated in the following account...

A group of girls was chased by several hungry bears. The girls, to escape, climbed a rock and hastily prayed to the Great Spirit for salvation. The Great Spirit, hearing the prayers, made the rock beneath the girls rise heavenward to take them out of reach. The hungry bears discovered that the new formation was too steep for them to climb. They stretched skyward in frustration, leaving deep claw marks on each side of what would someday be known as Devils Tower. The girls, having reached the sky, became the stars known as the Pleiades.

Devils Tower, in the years following the first viewings of the popular movie *Close Encounters of the Third Kind* that employed this setting, saw an increase in tourism. Each summer, hundreds of expert climbers, having attained a permit for ascent, utilize the Tower's cracks to help them reach the summit. We saw several of them working slowly toward the heights on our morning visit. As impressive as the spectacle seemed for this ultimate rockpile, I preferred to think about a gentler, safer way to reach the heights. I remembered a lazy stonefly on the pinnacle of a streamside cairn, not far from the blossom of a wildflower.

Like an Old-Fashioned Naturalist

All the environments I ever visited were not only distinct in themselves but shaded off into the unseen and the unfinished. Human isolation from the rest of life on a scale the modern world has made possible is inadmissible in the rest of nature.

– John Hay

1

Wildness is a part of nature that is simultaneously outside of our collective skins and at the very core of us. Wildness is essential for a healthy life on Earth; and it survives us even though all too many people try to hide it or relegate wildness into something that can be controlled. Although, personally, I've tried to live a lifestyle that embraces the wild, I'm quick to acknowledge that this state of being is so intricate and complex that humankind will always be sparring with it one way or another.

I could try to speak for wildness anywhere I find it: in the mountains or oceans, for example, or in the weedy portions of our gardens, cities and dreams. As a one-time student of psychology and as a naturalist today, I could try to speak of wildness for the simple reason that it's there—the wilderness surrounds us even though humankind has fought to disrupt it, to erase it, or in some way to control it, for our benefit. And in as much as we have never fully managed to subdue or dominate the wildness that surrounds us, we have been unable to fathom the distant shores of wildness in the human psyche.

Modern humanity is about 40-thousand-years old, give or take a few millennia. For most of this period, we have been hunter-gatherers, with the last 10 thousand years devoted to a slow shift into agriculture and urbanism, along with a growing penchant for technology. We get swept up in the changes and have a constant need for assessment of our actions. We confront the wild and look for ways to make our confrontation easier and less problematic.

Humans may labor exhaustively to buffer the wild with layers of technology, but the Paleolithic hunter-gatherer-fisherman with spear-sharp senses will remain inside each one of us. We can blow ourselves to kingdom come like chaff in the wind, but the seeds of wildness will remain, ready to renew the long journey into climax.

To acknowledge that the seeds of wildness will outlast us all may be a comforting thought, but it shouldn't mean that we resign ourselves to a life of social or political inactivity. Wilderness, or the many aspects of wild nature, can inspire us to create new ideas or works of art or science that, in turn, improve our lives and the health of our environment.

I draw inspiration from the wild in places like the Adirondacks or the backwoods of Yellowstone National Park, or I can draw it indirectly from a textbook or computer screen. For my money, there's no better place for inspiration than direct experience out-of-doors.

My writing as a naturalist often mirrors an experience in the wild. I take pleasure speaking for the wildness found in fly-fishing, walking, hiking, and other outdoor pursuits. Immersion in the natural realm is healthy, of course, and we go there because the world inspires us to enter that fold from which we came.

I like to find poetry in the world, in the elements surrounding us, waiting for connection and interpretation. I like to translate what is raw and flex it into ordinary words. That process, I suppose, is one facet of my job as naturalist. We all have personal frameworks in the world of nature, but all too many of us have forgotten our framework or allowed the social world to smash it. We have ways of realigning our humanity, however, with the history of our kind and with our hope for future days. As a naturalist, I try to do my small part allowing the lands and waters to assist our realignment. They speak directly and to the point. They speak the poetry of life.

2

I hardly qualify as a naturalist, considering my formal education. My degrees in psychology and elementary education don't go very far in giving me the science that's required in the deep study of the environment. What I know is what I've learned not only in the various schools that I've attended but also from what's interested me and spurred my curiosity from pre-school onward to this moment when I write. I call myself a self-learned naturalist, an amateur, because the term is one of the few nice names I can call myself.

When I consider the old-school naturalist, as opposed to the nature specialist of today, I think of someone like John Burroughs or Edwin Way Teale, two very different writers, both successful in what they studied and wrote about. Teale and Burroughs, plus a host of other early American naturalists, were capable of capturing what one historian has referred to as "the glorious, unspecialized freedom" found in outdoor studies. Thinking of the old-school naturalists in general, I suppose they share some characteristics that might be useful for aspiring naturalists who have no field of specialty.

An inherent curiosity and appreciation of nature is a basic characteristic of these individuals and it's probably a requisite trait for anyone who wants to share a love for the environment. An ability to demonstrate initiative and to derive enjoyment from outdoor activities is useful, as is an ability to *connect* with people. These are bottom-line characteristics of the naturalist for which no formal training is required, and I like to think that I have qualified in this regard, but it really doesn't matter. I just write and hope the message resonates.

3

Ants on a rock are like people on Earth. They crawl over the rounded surfaces pursuing whatever they must. They dominate those surfaces and subdue all other creatures. I step back from the rock that I investigate and settle into a wooden chair that's close to the fire-ring. I watch the ants. I have a place where I can do this freely and quietly, a special outdoor spot I call the "rec room" where I sidestep all the mayhem in the world and try to think in peace—or choose to not think at all. In my opinion, everyone needs to have a simple time-out place, an equivalent "rec room" of the mind.

I sit around the campfire ring and think about a small community in northern Pennsylvania, not far from here where I write. Families are forced to leave their homes because the hydrofracking industry is expanding through the region and wants their location for the construction of a major work site. The fracking industry has an upper hand in Pennsylvania, but the small-town residents have barricaded the streets near their trailer court to prevent entry by corporate representatives. The residents are furious and refuse to leave their homes. These people are financially destitute, in debt, and living in an area where housing prices are exorbitant, about three times the amount they were before a recent influx of workers for the fracking industry. I see ants on the rock at their barricades. Although there's probably more to the issue than I'm able to surmise, I wish the defenders well.

In the relative safety of this rec room I can hear the creek burbling 30 feet down the path. The evening robins sing the last of their territorial songs. A black bear ambles through a clearing just beyond my view. And soon the first fireflies will appear. There isn't much I can do to help a world in need of justice; I am ant-sized on the rough sphere of the night, but at least I have a voice.

I sit near the fire-ring at home and think about the larger fires raging through the western forestlands.

I've grown fond of many high-country sites where I've spent time in recent summers—forests now endangered due to drought and climate change, to poor management techniques, to arsonists and fools, and to lightning strikes. Forest fires are a natural occurrence in the scheme of things, necessary for survival of certain plants and animals, but the current scale of the forest fires is worrisome. I feel for the homeowners involved, for the wildlife and its habitats enflamed, and even for my own plans to investigate the wilderness in days to come. There's a lot that's going up in smoke; and the ants seethe over the rock.

If we're like ants on the rock, we probably try to do what's right. I recalled some words and thoughts sent to me by a friend: "We're lucky guys, whether we realize it or not." The gist of what my friend was saying is that goodness may consist of having family and friends, of having work plus an appreciation by others, of having access to the wild. Sitting with a comfortable fire late in the day, I acknowledged that the sentiment seems true—we were lucky; it was good despite all the problems and distractions cast off from the world. To prove it, I would help the darkness blanket the remaining fire-glow emanating from the center of the rec room; I would bid the ants goodnight, wherever they had gone, and walk back to the house.

A giant moth came to face me at a window. *Polyphemus* is a silk moth with purple eye-spots on the hindwings. Pressed against a windowpane, this tan-colored creature had spread its wings as if relaxed, but it seemed to stare right into the heart of me as if I was the source of light itself. I saw it as a possible messenger from beyond the dark, beyond the realms of science and the viewpoint of a lepidopterist. Polyphemus seemed to say that the ants were all asleep, the world that I knew was sleeping, and I had better get some sleep as well. I gave it the veil of poetry. I reasoned that a dash of anthropomorphism wouldn't hurt an old-time naturalist in the story that he tells.

4

Crows have been drawing my attention lately. Driving along the Ridge Road in the afternoon I've watched hundreds of them feeding and cavorting over freshly manured fields. These most intelligent of birds, these common and adaptable, ubiquitous creatures seem a blessing and a curse to humankind, and I must admit I've got mixed feelings about them. I've cursed them when they roosted by the hundreds over village parking lots and covered our newest vehicle with so much excrement that it took three-plus carwash entries to scrub all the shit from the paint and windows. And I had to thank them recently when it seemed their cawing was an invitation to begin a walk in their direction for a lesson to be learned. A naturalist, a student of landscapes and perception, might find that crows speak in motions, guttural sounds, and wrinkles of the air. The corvid messages, if we dare to heed them, speak of mystery and surprise, of nihilism and hope, and of getting back to basics.

There was a murder of crows on the hills and it was noisy (getting more so as the winter season progresses toward spring). I took the liberty of translating the crow commotion, the birds' connection to me, as saying it was time to start tying flies again. It was a leap of faith, perhaps, to go from crow noise to the tying of feathers on a trout hook, but why not take it? Crows are known to be capable of recognizing individual humans (not that any crow has ever singled me out as a person of significance) and they're capable of figuring the simplest of math problems (as I usually am, if I've had a good night's sleep), so why not have them point out the obvious: a new fly-fishing season was approaching fast, and I'd better get back to the tying bench.

I thought about a favorite line from the late farmer-poet, W. W. Christman, of upstate New York: "You crows upon the reddening hill, / Cease wrangling for a while, be still." The image of a reddening hill reminded me of a small red painting that I purchased in New Mexico about 10 years earlier. "Crow Messengers" is a watercolor by the artist David Gary Suazo. Today I took it from the wall and studied this reflection by the Native American painter. It was like a daydream when I closed my eyes. Crows came in from the cold and settled around me like the night. Two of the birds seemed to have a message bundled around their wings, a message tied in white ribbon. Crows can drive you crazy if you let them, if you stay inactive, so I shook them off, replaced the painting on my kitchen wall and headed for the tying vise.

I tied a handful of early season favorites, not exactly trout cuisine or works of art, just meat and potatoes on a hook. I also tied a bunch of wingless wet flies, soft-hackle patterns whose lineage reaches back to the merry days of fifteenth-century England. Patterns like the Partridge & Orange, the North Country Spider, and the Orange Fish Hawk. For all my years of fly-fishing I had largely ignored these patterns, so it was time to get familiar with their recipes and use. My calendar still said February, but the old-time naturalist in me, the generalist whose traditions date back to the time of Aristotle, felt the strangely warm weather and heard the crows rasp, "Move it, old fella; get back to the basics and prepare; refuse to be obsolete!"

Again, the words of W. W. Christman: "The clamorous crows! How basic and strangely human/ To cry their fate of death, voice love and hate--/ Long living gives them wisdom, the acumen/ To make no truce with man or beast or fate."

5

At least several renowned fishing writers have described Pennsylvania's Rock Run, a tributary of Lycoming Creek, as the most beautiful, spectacular and picturesque trout stream in the state. One author went so far as placing Rock Run among the most scenic waters in America; and *Backpacker* magazine rated the stream in 2009 as the "#1 swimming hole" in the U.S., which certainly assured that the run would rise from the valleys of anonymity. Whatever the case, Rock Run is not a secret held from fishermen or nature buffs.

This well-named stream had been on my bucket-list of creeks to fly-fish for a decade, ever since first reading of its beauty. The stream tumbles from the McIntyre Wild Area of the Loyalsock State Forest in north-central PA, a stream with a steep gradient, with walls and ledges, waterfalls and swirling potholes, with chute-like channels boring through solid bedrock, and with water typically so clear that you might see trout hugging the bottom of pools at depths of 20 feet or more.

The run, whose mid-section waters average about 30 feet wide in summer, also has some braids, or chutes, narrow enough for a man to step across. The stream, well-scoured, has virtually no sediment, and gravel can be scarce. Insect hatches and sizeable trout are less than what you might suspect, but walking the run is a pleasurable experience.

When I found some internet videos extolling this trout stream as a place for family swimming parties and even for kayak adventures in spring, I figured that I better make my introduction quickly before the stream's popularity killed off its appeal. Rock Run does have some environmental protection by virtue of the state forest on its banks, but the stream's security seems limited. As the writer Ed Abbey once declared, it's not enough to understand the world of nature; we naturalists and citizens of the planet also need to increase our efforts to defend and preserve it.

There was another reason that I finally got around to visiting the stream. I had read about Elizabeth S. Benjamin (1829-1907) who lived in the village of Ralston at the mouth of Rock Run, and I wanted to learn more about her life as a fly-tier. According to eminent fly-fishing historians such as Paul Schullery, Benjamin is the first American woman to have tied flies commercially. Although some of her trout flies are displayed in the American Museum of Fly-Fishing in Manchester, Vermont, very little is known about her life.

With luck, I might find a clue about Elizabeth Benjamin's existence in Ralston. I made a casual inspection of an old cemetery above the banks of the Lycoming but found no family name of Benjamin among the aging stones. Elizabeth had studied the insects that emerged from trout streams near her home and had watched the habits of anglers in what was once a popular gathering place for those who fished for large brook trout.

Some of the more renowned naturalists of the nineteenth-century are reputed to have held a great variety of interests within the scope of nature sciences. That variety of interest, ranging from astronomy to zooplankton, seems much wider than the typical interest held by modern scientists. Today our specialized fields with fast-paced calculations and computerized analyses seem a world apart. I had to wonder if the fly-tying Benjamin was a generalist akin to our early nature writers or more in line with the narrow focus of present-day specialists. I had to wonder if maybe I was being too romantic when considering the possibilities. Elizabeth Benjamin may have been no more than another opportunist—a poor country woman smart enough to see commercial leverage by offering the trout fishers something new.

Benjamin, along with her son who gathered tying feathers from local birds, and her husband who helped in various undisclosed capacities, established a lucrative fly-tying business in the valley as early as 1853. Today I found no indication of a fly-fishing interest whatsoever. Other than a bald eagle that I saw flying over the Lycoming, the only other positive sign I found was in the local general store.

The woman who clerked at this location, hearing that I was about to climb the mountain roadway for my introduction to Rock Run, pointed out a small pack of wet-fly leaders built for casting three artificial flies at a time—a practice that had once been standard for fishing with submerged trout flies. She inquired if I knew who might have built those leaders. The store had acquired them long ago, and the woman wanted more of them to sell. I had no idea who might have built those 7'6" and those 9-foot leaders complete with dropper tippets, but ever curious about such matters, I purchased a 9-footer for later use on the Lycoming.

The weather forecast for my debut had given a 20-percent chance of rain, which sounded pretty good until the chance became a 100-percent certainty of morning-long precipitation. As I climbed the narrow gravel road (apparently the day's first visitor), I worried that the rain might drop a tree or heavy branch across the road and cause a problem, but when I saw another intrepid soul parking his vehicle then heading for the run, I decided it was now or never. I would do some wet-wading for trout.

The other visitor went swimming in the rain and took underwater photographs in the plunge-pool of a waterfall. It was his first visit to the stream, as well. I stepped carefully on the slick, treacherous rocks and tried to hook a stocked or wild trout in the cold, clear water of the run.

I spooked a few fish, but for now the trout had little to fear from my appearance. Maybe in the fall, when the foliage explodes with color, I would have more luck. Maybe then, with a little more exploration under my belt, I'd be able to judge whether this beautiful stream is truly more spectacular than any other fished in Pennsylvania.

6

The clouds were building over Cedar Run and its forested gorge. The afternoon was looking good for fishing in the low clear water, but the trout weren't having anything to do with the small flies that I offered them. I paused to take a picture of Joe-Pye-weed flowers blooming at head-level on the banks of the run. It was then that I saw the first Blue-winged Olives fluttering from the stream. I tied on an imitation of the little mayfly and watched the brook and brown trout race out from their hiding spots to try their luck.

"Eye-to-eye contact with nature is the truest of experiences," wrote the old-school naturalist, Ann Zwinger, who passed away in 2014. I felt the truth of Zwinger's statement while standing in the stream and wondering about Joe Pye (Jopi) for whom Joe-Pye-weed is named. Ostensibly, Joe was a Native American doctor living in New England during the 1800s. Little is known about him, so I had an opportunity to think creatively about his life. Joe Pye was a healer capable of applying extracts of *Eupatorium purpureum* and curing patients suffering from typhus fever and other ailments.

I was looking all around my place on Cedar Run but seemed to focus on Joe-Pye-weed. Butterflies cavorted there and stopped for blooms of boneset, goldenrod and aster. I'd been standing still for minutes when I saw a bulge in the shallow pool. A large brown trout cruised by. As the trout shifted downstream toward the far bank of the run, its wake cut cleanly through the riffles, and I uttered something like, "Holy… Jopi!"

I'm not one to call the Joe-Pye bloom a "weed." No. I call it a pale pink flower, an herb that grows well along streams and forest edges. The plant can grow taller than a pro-basketball player and can make itself at home in flower gardens. It's said that if you crush the flower (please be kind), the fragrance given resembles light vanilla… Man, I love vanilla.

Retreating from Cedar Run, I took the Joe-Pye essence with me to the hotel restaurant at Slate Run village. I forgot about it while I ate a tasty meal and lubricated my interior with a Two-Hearted Ale. Then I took a short hike into the Slate Run gorge. By the time I reached a favorite trout pool, I figured I had an hour of fishing before the night closed in.

I was casting with my new fly rod, laying out a looping line across calm water to the faster riffles of a pool, when I had the feeling that I wasn't alone. Earlier I had seen an angler passing upstream from my view, but with a glance up and down the run, all I saw now was another splashy rise-form given by a heavy trout.

Several fish were feeding at the surface, but I couldn't decipher what they were targeting. There were no obvious hatches occurring. No spinners graced the air above the stream. There might have been small ants or midges touching the water, but even my tiniest imitation didn't get more than a quick inspection and a snub.

Something other than bugs and trout food hung in the air. I turned sharply toward the pine and hemlock trees behind me on the bank. There he was—a middle-aged fisherman sitting on a tree stump as he watched me in the stream. I felt a little sheepish but gave the guy a wave, and the fellow kindly responded.

I remembered Joe Pye. It seemed as if the Joe-Pye-spirit had recalled me to the dance. Waiting for some words to leave my mouth, I made a few more casts to the head of the pool and watched the drifting fly. Then, turning sharply toward the fisherman on the stump, I asked, "How did you do downstream? Any luck?"

"No, I had one fish come up, but I missed it."

I made another cast, waited a minute, then asked one final question: "Would you like to fish this pool? The trout are picky as hell, but you're more than welcome to try."

"No," he said. "I just like watching someone who knows what he's doing."

I was speechless. I glanced at the trees beyond the head of the pool. Was there someone in there unbeknownst to me? Someone who knew what he was *doing*? I just waved and went on fishing, and several minutes later the tree-stump sitter rose and yelled, "Good luck!"

It might have been an incarnation of Joe Pye, someone other than me, an old-fashioned naturalist, perhaps, who shouted "Thank you!" in return. I don't know. The first deep shades of darkness were beginning to blur the sense of wonder while effacing the variety and richness in the world. September nights come quickly to a trout stream in the gorge.

Portrait of the Chinook as an Old Man

1

I saw the king salmon, the Chinook, shiver into the pool and come to rest. He was 30 feet away, with deep water and variant current speeds between us. The hunter's challenge came to the fore, even though I knew that the traveling king, if subdued, would be released to die alone.

I didn't want him for a photograph to prove that I could beat a 25-pound wrestler. I didn't need a victory to massage a hoary ego. All I consciously wanted was to make a good cast, to know I did my best, and to somehow assimilate a little of the salmon's awesome strength.

He didn't want the white Woolly Bugger or an Olive Egg-sucking Leech. They didn't irritate him enough to strike. "Dark flies for dark waters," I recalled, so changed my pattern for a black streamer with a chartreuse head. The change absorbed the outside world to nothingness. What had been seen was gone from view; what had been heard fell into silence. The whistling of a white-throated sparrow, the rustling of a cornfield and of willow leaves became like whispers less substantial than a memory.

In my experience, many eastern anglers disregard or hate Old Man Chinook. He's not as classy as a two-foot brown trout or a shimmering steelhead. And he's dying—he might be here to spawn and to make his one and only run for glory, but he'll rot and stink the water; he's a Great Lakes tributary breeder at the end of his life's cycle.

Even though we're now a few decades from the horrors of the snagging era for salmon in New York (a period which I'm glad to have missed), a lot of anglers still believe that Old Man Chinook will not strike at a lure. He's only good for snagging, if he's good for anything at all. In this case, I pinched another split-shot to the leader, just above the fly. The streamer would descend to the proper depth, to eye level, and not be swept above him by conflicting currents or be whisked to any part of that great body other than the lip.

The old guy bit; the jaws grabbed the black streamer the way he's taken fly after fly cast by me and other anglers through our many autumns of pursuit. Old Man Chinook and Pacific salmon in general have had their place here in the Great Lakes drainage since their introduction to supplant the crash of native fish in the middle of the twentieth-century. It can be a challenge to fool a king or Coho salmon on its spawning run, but the fish will hit an artificial lure presented with a tease.

The big fish was a powerhouse of energy, arcing an 8-weight fly rod into worrisome stress, its fighting butt boring into the abdomen of a gray-haired predator along the bank. Ten minutes later I slid him to a pull-out downstream of the place where it all began; I'm exhausted by the struggle and pleased to be alive. The fish's length, measured along the 9-foot rod, was 40 inches, and his color, green with black spots along the back from head to tail, recharged that part of me that had drained off in the struggle, renewed my energy the way a fresh-run, fair-hooked salmon always does.

I've caught larger fish than Old Man Chinook but, nonetheless, he looks impressive. He might be the Rodney Dangerfield of salmonids by getting the short end of respect in fishermen's eyes, but we've got to hand it to him—he can be a freight train on the angler's line. He's a kingpin when he's fresh-run from the lake or ocean, an old guy who'll remind us that his kind is special. Recently, a friend of mine was fishing the Clearwater River in Idaho when he found a Nez Perce inscription on a rock that said, "If we take care of salmon, the salmon will care for us." Yeah, Old Man Chinook gets around.

2

Transformation in the river of life can be as dramatic as a landslide sweeping across a channel or as subtle and degrading as discovery of a new leak in a pair of fishing waders. As for the latter kind of change, I should have seen it coming…

At first there was just dampness on the legs after fishing a trout stream in Virginia, then came the full-blown flood in cold New York—my one-year-old Field & Stream waders were shot. I had studied the landlocked salmon/brown trout river, flowing high and slightly turbid, and decided that the late-November water looked inviting. The air temperature was 36 degrees F., and the water that began to fill my wader legs was slightly warmer. When I quit fishing two hours later, I looked at a frozen foot removed from a water-logged boot and noted its resemblance to a blood-drawn turnip. Good god, I thought, is that item really mine?

For two foolish hours of casting I had felt like a sinking canoe, with perforated waist-highs letting in cold water. I was only somewhat disappointed, though, since the year-old waders had served me well. If that sounds as though they didn't last me long enough, I did get more than a hundred rugged outings from them, and even if I'd paid double their cost for a sturdier pair of waders, I doubt I could have done much better. I am rough on my equipment.

I should have seen more fish than I did, considering the recent flush of rain, but I didn't find them till about the time I nearly turned to ice, perhaps due to the water's sudden depth and darkness. I recall that at one point I could peer down at my foot in the river and consider the possibility of it being a spawning trout.

Several landlocked salmon and maybe a brown trout swam into view. Big ones. But it took a while before I finally got a hook-up with a salmon. The fish shot off downstream, turned broadside in the rapids and broke away. I consoled myself by thinking the fish was probably foul-hooked hopelessly, but then, wasn't that a fin that seemed to wave goodbye as the body sank from view? The fin's wave could have been a handkerchief dancing from the window of a bus departing from a Greyhound station. See you later, buddy. Come back when your feet are thawed, when you've ditched those road-killed waders. And don't bother trying to write about me, either. I'm a non-event; I'm just fake news.

I couldn't believe I was listening to a fish that wasn't there, responding in a frozen way, deluded into thinking that a long-gone salmon could be so mean-spirited. I would write of him if I wanted to. After all, this was only fishing, and he, gone or not, was part of the karmic record, one more element of my experience. I did thank the salmon, though, for calling my waders "roadkill." I would order a new pair right away, and before I'd realize it, I'd be fishing in the cold December snow, complaining about my foolishness like a bear caught wandering in the chill of a dying year.

3

"Walt Franklin on the Stream" is a wood carving that my wife gave me as a Christmas present years ago. The sculpture, an example of Pennsylvania folk art, was produced by David Castano, a full-time wood carver from Potter County, PA.

Castano's approach to working with a knife might be construed as an attempt to represent an individual in the context of family and work traditions. According to the artist, his wooden figures reflect the value and diversity of workers in America. He was once commissioned to carve the figures of nine surviving mine workers rescued in 2002 from the Que Creek coal disaster in southwestern Pennsylvania.

Since fly-fishing isn't usually thought to be a part of America's work traditions, I was fortunate to be considered a suitable subject for the carver's time. But wait a minute—can't fun be part of the *work* experience, too? Let's look at this example…

Winter had been present for a while, but on Winter Solstice, the astronomical gun-start for the season, rain was on tap for the region, and the temperature was rising quickly. Since the weather hadn't registered above the freezing mark in more than two weeks, I wanted to fly-fish if the signs were good, so I packed a couple of rods for a drive to the Kettle Creek Tackle Shop. The plan was to fish, if possible, and to drop off one rod that I'd broken in November.

Phil Baldacchino's shop near Hammersley Fork is a favorite fly and tackle center in my region, and the owner had agreed to make a replacement tip for a bamboo rod that he had sold. Phil was quick to show some of the latest fly rods he had built, cool fiberglass and bamboo instruments. I stood there in the narrow aisles of the shop as he handed me one rod after another, expertly providing the statistics for each one. In the dim glow of the quiet shop, I was like an old salmon that had found his natal river, like a kid aboard the Polar Express that pushed across the Northern Lights.

I was there only to deliver a broken rod and maybe to buy a few small items, but the fun that came from looking over all the new stuff started to reveal the dark side of the sport. It began to feel like work. Putting thumb prints on a gorgeous spacer carved from box elder and testing the "speed" of various rod tapers, for example, wasn't easy, but I thought, what the hell. It was the Winter Solstice; why not stand back and enjoy?

Returning home in the rain, I slowed the car at numerous bridge crossings and threw a long eye to the widening streams. The waters were rising from a sudden snow-melt. Road slush was accumulating and preventing a safe stop, so I limited my day's work to the job description of a stream monitor. Difficult labor, maybe, but somebody had to do it.

At home, I took David Castano's carving from the shelf. I turned it upside down and read the statue's title at the bottom. "Walt Franklin on the Stream." I took it to our creekside by the waterfall and stood the statue at the water's edge, the way a kid might play with sticks beside a pool. The carving looked right at home there by the creek. I thought about the fishing creel constructed at my side. Although I'd never worn a wicker basket even in the formative years of youth, the notion of it smacked of *tradition*, so was fine with me. The scene looked almost celebratory in the rain. A gift from the past gave me enjoyment in the present. I even had a fish pulled from the water, lively in the air.

4

About five years ago I read an email message from my son that read, "If dad had a time machine, this fish would be a *lifer*, for certain!" When I opened the accompanying link, I learned of a salmonid I had never heard of before. And I was curious…

Oncorhynchus rastrosus, the so-called saber-toothed salmon, once inhabited the region we now refer to as the Pacific Northwest. It lived through the late Miocene era (about 13 million years ago) until the Pleistocene (about four million years ago). It took a while before I finally got an email on this subject (much appreciated)—on what is surely the largest salmon yet unleashed upon an angler's dreams.

The saber-tooth, named for the impressive canines on the upper jaw, is said to have grown upward of 2.7 meters, or about nine-feet long. The large teeth were useful to the males competing on the spawning ground. Large teeth aside, studies suggest that *rastrosus* was a plankton eater and had relatively few teeth compared to its modern relatives. Fossils found on upland sites in Oregon and California reveal that the big fish was anadromous. The saber-tooth, like its closest living relative, the sockeye salmon, matured in the ocean and then traveled to the rivertops to spawn and die.

This salmon is an inspiration to poet, angler and ichthyologist. It doesn't take much for imagination to get suited when approaching *rastrosus*—a seven-foot monster with a kype to kill, leaping through autumn riffles, rocketing over average waterfalls en route to the forested heights, resting in limpid pools, and dropping into redds the size of Subarus.

What fly rod would I need to handle a saber-tooth? A 12-weight or a 14? Something more powerful, surely, than the eight or 9-weight used for Old Man Chinook. And what fly patterns would I use? But wait… Isn't there a more basic question to be asked before we think about the tackle? Like, how do we get to saber-tooth country in the first place?

Okay, so I'd need a time machine, of sorts. But since I can't even figure out computers, let alone an updated vehicle of the H. G. Wells variety, I'd need to find some ticket yet unknown, something so basic and unscientific that it's probably right before my nose. Something like another swill of Porkslap Farmhouse Ale or a shot of Old No. 7. Better yet, a long-gone 60's psychedelic trip, or perhaps a straighter route like teleportation.

Ah, to shape-shift through the ages! To catch saber-tooth salmon with a fly rod, Old Man Chinook on steroids... The human brain, clogged by hubris and a warped ego, is a sad thing to behold, a hopeless artifact, and yet without it we are nowhere; we are nothing if we can't give thanks to dreams.

5

It was Squonk season in northern Pennsylvania, in the great forests near Cedar Run where I've been fishing of late. The Squonk was first discovered in the hemlock woods of the region in the late 1800s when exhausted lumberjacks would sit around the fire on cold winter nights, drinking whatever made them feel good, then conjuring the likes of a Squonk for their own pleasure.

It's Squonk season in the Northwoods where this shape-shifter is known to have various forms and personalities, from monstrous and pathetic to silly or downright frightening. No matter what it looks like, the Squonk has certain character traits. It's said to be secretive and shy, often so ugly that it weeps about its own appearance. It's been known to resemble a small bird with a long bill or, at another extreme, a geezer of a salmon that has spawned-out to be dressed in its fungal robe of death. One account describes the Squonk as a clumsy warthog with blemished skin, and another literary reference tells about an insecure spirit, a loser that's ashamed to show its face, a sniveler through the long nights of fall and winter.

The hunting season for Squonk in Pennsylvania runs from October 1st to the start of the firearms season for deer and bear. A hunter is allowed one Squonk per year; it's got to be tagged and then reported to the Game Commission. I've never hunted for one, myself, but I understand that *L. dissolvens*, in whatever form it takes, is easy prey for those who seek it. Ostensibly, all a hunter needs to do is follow a tear-stained trail along a stream or through the forest.

Apparently, the greatest challenge for a hunter is to bag the Squonk before it's cornered and begins to weep. Failing to get the creature into a corner may result in dissolution from a pool of tears. J. P. Wentling, an early twentieth-century lumberman, captured a live Squonk at Cedar Run and stuffed it in a bag. Hiking toward his camp, Wentling felt the bag go suddenly weightless. Untying the rope that enclosed the quarry, Wentling peeked inside... Imagine his shock—the Squonk had dissolved into briny fluid.

The Squonk first appeared in print with *Fearsome Creatures of the Lumberwoods* (1910), by William T. Cox. The great contemporary novelist, Jorge Luis Borges, featured the Squonk in his *Book of Imaginary Beings*. The rock band, Steely Dan, included a Squonk reference in one of its songs, and the band Genesis recorded a song called "Squonk" for an album released in 1976. Though seldom seen, the Squonk may seem ubiquitous.

I encountered the animal on a cold October morning along Cedar Run, and when I least expected one. I was casting a dry fly, wading gingerly through a riffle, when I heard a sobbing noise that I first mistook for the babbling of water over stone. I saw a fat gray bird, the size of a chicken, stumble into the streamside grasses, crying uncontrollably then slipping out of view.

Curious, I approached the point of disappearance and found it strangely quiet. A long brown serpent appeared on the surface of the stream. When I say "long," I mean 20 to 25-feet in length. The huge snake slithered toward me with a tail-first, serpentine motion that took a couple of seconds to be recognized as one of the best hallucinations I have had in years. What had likely been my first real sighting of a Squonk was now a scaly vine tethered to the alders. The Squonk had done more than simply dissolve into tears. It had morphed into a great rope of tightly bound leaves and grasses swaying like an anaconda on a tropical stream.

Why would it do such a thing? Did it think that I would shoot it? All I carried was a bamboo fishing rod. I suppose it could have morphed into Old Man Chinook if the setting had been a Great Lakes tributary. As it was, the swaying vine on Cedar Run became a link to the whiskey minds and lumber camps, to the long cold evenings of another time.

Winter Rose

1

After my mother died at year's end, the emotional roller-coaster ride for the family was leavened happily a few days later by the marriage of my son in the brighter atmosphere of northern Virginia. The life-affirming action taken by the young couple in Virginia was like seeing the first new light of winter edging through the darkness in a season of holidays. The poetic spin I gave it likened the event to witnessing a freshly cut winter rose. And speaking of roses—at the family gathering, I had an opportunity to fly-fish once again on the upper Rose River in Shenandoah National Park.

Any chance to fish comfortably during the winter season is, for me, a bonus, so I scrambled for the water. We were staying in Warrenton, Virginia where the air temperature was mild the day after Christmas, so the drive to the Rose was pleasant and easy. My son and I were greeted by a bald eagle flying over the Rappahannock River Valley as we made our way to the Blue Ridge and prepared for a short hike and a fishing jaunt into the wilds of Shenandoah.

The Rose, just inside the park boundary, is a boulder-choked stream with a steep gradient, lovely water where you can fish for wild brook trout on a catch-and-release basis with artificial flies or lures. The winter stream was low and clear, the footing treacherous along the rocky banks, and the fish seemed few and far between. Based on my experience along the Blue Ridge waterways a month earlier, this venture reinforced my suspicions that a lot of trout had moved upstream during the hot, dry summer in search of cooler water, and that the fish had yet to drop back to the lower section of the mountains. This was purely conjecture at the time. Right or wrong, fishing was what I needed. Just a couple of winter hours in the wild, with a couple of beautiful brook trout to tighten the line by taking a nymph or a Glo-Bug, like a red rose in a soul bouquet.

2

Old Woodenhead (my alter ego on cold December streams) was on the Allegheny River by noon. The weather had warmed a bit, became more seasonal, with an air temperature peaking at the freezing mark. Old Woodenhead had decided that winter fly-fishing was certainly an exercise in patience and layered clothing. Fingers freeze while attending to snags and tangles. Every action, whether short line casting or reeling in a stubborn fish, is accomplished as if with wooden hands.

He was not alone there by the river. An army of eleven orange-clad deer hunters advanced across a forested slope nearby. For safety's sake, Old Woodenhead had added a fluorescent-orange vest over his usual Orvis tans. He may have grumbled, wondering why he bothered with this masochistic behavior but, when all was cursed and settled, he would have it no other way. To fish in winter was to feel alive.

He was on a river pool with depth and more than a few large trout. The one side of the pool from which he could cast had 10 to 15-feet of thin ice on the surface. He watched the shadowy forms of trout shift on the river bottom out beyond the ice. Casting an Egg fly to the open water, he allowed the lure to sink and slowly drift. Eventually, a trout grabbed the fly and rose toward the edge of the ice. Fish on!

Old Woodenhead kept the line tight while scrambling downstream to the tail-end of the pool. He didn't want the ice to sever his connection. Gaining the proper position, he worked the fish into the net and removed the hook. The brown trout measured 17 inches long. He took two photos and returned the catch, adding holiday wishes to all with fin or fur or feather.

Each December, Old Woodenhead skates fearlessly on the thin ice of reality, resuming his quest for fun and knowledge in unusual ways. A traditionalist, he fly-fishes, hikes and makes a nuisance of himself to those he loves and cherishes, but much of what he does in winter occurs on the snow and ice. No one will accuse him of being graceful or particularly wise, but he means well, and, by god, he even catches a trout now and then.

3

A winter rose, almost by definition, won't remain in bloom for long, its petals doomed to fall the way a sad thought enters the mind and corrugates a pathway to the heart. It's time for me to clear those petals and grieve, just briefly, for the long-departed passenger pigeon.

Ectopistes migratorius was once the most abundant wild bird in North America and, perhaps, in the world. It's been said that more than a quarter of all the birds in North America in the 1800s were this powder-blue pigeon that was larger than a mourning dove and most closely related to the western band-tailed pigeon.

Many of us have read of the enormous flocks of passenger pigeons that once passed through the skies of northeastern America in the nineteenth-century, but we can be certain that no one alive today has ever seen this fascinating bird. The last "wild pigeon" died in the Cincinnati Zoo in 1914.

Curious about the one-time presence of the passenger pigeon in my haunted neck of home, I checked into a little history book devoted to my Town of Greenwood, New York. The book called *Pioneer Life in Greenwood, 1888*, by Dennis McGraw, echoes the demise of the pigeon in a way that many local histories have. McGraw wrote:

> *On the upland, the timber was mostly beech and maple. The maple was a great help to the people as from them we got our sugar and molasses. The beech used to furnish feed to fat our pork and to call the pigeons to nest, which supplied us with young squabs. They used to nest there in an early day, every bearing year. Once when at work in the sugar camp on the head of Bennett's Creek, about five o'clock in the evening, we discovered pigeons in clouds; there*

were so many of them they fairly darkened the sky, and they kept coming until after dark when the tree tops were black with them. After nightfall we thought we could get a large quantity of them by felling the trees one against the other, but in that we were disappointed, for as soon as we struck a tree with an ax they would flutter off. We never got one pigeon that night, but what we got was better. They nested in the big marsh and we got any quantity of squabs as fat as butter. People came from a great distance with wagons and barrels and fell acres of timber to get them. It was a sight to see, and one that we shall never see in this country.

The passenger pigeon was annihilated by over-hunting and habitat destruction. A migratory Ontario flock was described in a literary reference as "one mile wide, 300 miles long, taking 14 hours to pass a single point" which, if accurate, could have accounted for most of the estimated 3.5 billion pigeons in North America at the time. An avian holocaust, a systematic extermination of a species, loomed.

Pigeons were found to be good for feeding the nation's slaves and poor. Massive mechanized hunting methods were designed. Typically, birds flocked together for predator protection and lived in large colonies, sometimes building hundreds of nests in a single tree. The nesting trees were burned, sometimes with sulphur additives. Flocks were drawn down from the sky by use of a live but blinded "stool pigeon." Double-barreled shotguns could occasionally blast 60 pigeons at a time. At one Michigan site, boys were encouraged to kill upward of 50,000 roosting birds per day, for five months duration. You get the picture.

Studying local history can be enlightening, not only for the dour news about events such as this extinction, but for a wealth of entertaining and lighter news as well. Many people simply disregard the local. They have too much information at their fingertips already; they have busy schedules and bills to pay; the power mongers have stripped their lives of heritage and pride, etcetera. The fact that a lot of local history has been written poorly and contains uninteresting material doesn't help its cause, for sure, but for many people it is simply way too precious and unnecessary.

For the folks who care about history and its local aspects, though, the picture brightens. To get local and to take an interest in community and environment seems almost revolutionary, in a sense. I think of the ideas, beliefs and feelings that tore a new American spirit free from European tyranny in the eighteenth-century. Since then, through good times and bad, we've become a nation of extremely mobile and unsettled people with diminishing stakes in the past. We don't have time for romantic ruminations, don't have time to develop a sense of place or to see ourselves evolving in sustainable frameworks. We no longer wish to know the old ways, or to see ourselves as part of a natural community with interacting or dependent parts. Or do we?

Maybe I'm just seeing the black rose of history here, the dried and wrinkled hip of darker times. No doubt, our culture has absorbed important lessons stemming from mistakes made in the previous century or two but, listening to the news today, I still hear about the wars and disease, the ravages of pollution and technological mayhem, the injustice and the lies. I can hear this and still not wish to live in any other period.

The last wild passenger pigeon was said to be killed by an Ohio boy with a BB gun in 1900. The extinction would eventually arouse public interest in the conservation movement. The time would be ripe for the works of great environmental thinkers such as Rachel Carson and Aldo Leopold who, incidentally, would pay a public tribute to the passenger pigeon on a formerly large Wisconsin roosting site. Like a winter rose, our history lives and blooms within us for the viewing. As the poet T.S. Eliot once concluded, "The historical sense involves a perception not only of the pastness of the past, but of its presence also."

4

My top dozen reasons to fish the home river on New Year's Day (in no special order):

1—No hangover from the night before.
2—No reasons are necessary, but some "whys" may need to be articulated.
3—I'm not talking about the Florida Keys here, but the Genesee River in New York. "Support your local fishery."
4—I'm not a great football fan; I don't watch TV. Oddly, I'm still American.
5—There is no closed season here; the river's still free of ice, off-color, fishable as is.
6—You never know what a drifting streamer on a sinking line will tempt.

7—Your chances for catching a trout are better than winning the lottery, plus the misery of *waiting* is almost bearable.

8—On a day like this, there is no other madman in sight.

9—Although the rain will drive me off in 20 minutes, troutless, I can welcome Winter before it feels like serious Winter.

10—It's a good omen to fish the first day of the year (if not here, then someplace else).

11—I may be cold and numb but I'm upright and alive. The last cast of the day will feel so good!

12—The winter rose blooms at no other time. The fishing can only get better.

5

One day in early February I took a four-mile ramble in the Pine Creek Natural Area, aka the Pine Creek Gorge, or the Grand Canyon of Pennsylvania. I was on the canyon's Rail Trail following the mostly ice-covered waters of upper Pine Creek. The air was a crisp 23 degrees Fahrenheit although the sun was shining periodically, illuminating the snow and ice and several tracks of skiers and hikers.

I had total solitude in this 20-mile stretch of wildness flowing north to south at depths of nearly a thousand feet below the sandstone escarpments at each rim. My company was a great blue heron, a pileated woodpecker and an animal which I'll speak of in a minute, but I felt quite sheltered from the mundane world beyond. The "longest creek in America" was at my feet, and a vast state forestland embraced the cliffs just east and west of me.

According to a late twentieth-century report by the National Park Service, the Pine Creek Gorge Natural Area contains "superlative scenery, geological and ecological value, and is one of the finest examples of a deep gorge in the eastern United States." I agree with that assessment, and again felt the need to finally do some fly-fishing along the creek's Delayed Harvest water come April. I have visited the gorge on numerous occasions over the previous few decades but have never rafted its course from Ansonia to Blackwell or even traversed it with a fly rod or a bicycle along the popular Rail Trail.

There was no time like the present to become better acquainted. Whereas many people take a raft, canoe or kayak through the gorge when the water conditions are favorable, my own preference would be to bike the trail and pedal to a stop at each side-canyon to inspect its feeder stream for brook trout with a short four-piece rod. For now, however, walking was the way to go.

This natural area was a gift from the last Ice Age when the melting glacier thwarted Pine Creek's northward flow and reversed it through impressionable sandstone. The creek, re-routed, helped carve this complicated landscape of forested hills and gorges. This was wilderness until the late nineteenth-century logging boom occurred.

I was near Deadman Hollow, named for an early twentieth-century trapper whose decomposed body was discovered in a bear trap he had set. Earlier, the Iroquois and Susquehannock hunters had traveled the course for many years. In recent decades, the Jersey Shore, Pine Creek and Buffalo Railroad had traversed the gorge with freight and passenger service, forming the backbone of an industry that spread throughout the larger watershed.

The old growth forests were stripped bare by the early 1900s. Nothing was left but treetops which eventually fueled great fires that ravaged the land. Along with the floods that followed, there were landslides and erosion to the point of ecological ruin. The region took on the appearance of a northern desert.

Over the past century, however, the forests have regrown and much of the wildlife has returned. Although the wolves, elk and panthers are gone, the bears, otter, and eagles can be found; and wild trout thrive in many of Pine Creek's tributaries. Visitors arrive en masse to enjoy the state parks, hiking trails and waterways. Following the demise of the locomotive era, the Rail Trail opened in 1996 and has become quite popular with bikers, hikers, fishermen, and other recreationalists.

For this hike, I neglected to carry food and water due to my initial idea to walk but a short distance. I got thirsty after the first mile of rambling. I was at the point of scooping up snow when I heard the song of water from the rocks on my left. Water gushed out from a pipe thrusting from a cliff. Wonderful!

Returning to the trail, I glanced at an open stretch of Pine Creek water and saw a dark-furred animal poised along an edge of the ice. The eyes of a river otter met my own—my first good look at an otter in the East! I had seen the animal in several western states over the years, but this was special.

I wanted a photo, but those eyes, unblinking, told me that my chances were slim. I positioned my walking stick, slowly removed my gloves, and tried to prepare the camera. Looking up, I saw that the otter was gone—no photo this time, but I took some pictures of the animal's unusual tracks across the snow.

Otters were reintroduced to the Pine Creek Natural Area from other regions of the wild several decades earlier, and they are doing well. These fast-swimming fish-eaters require pristine water conditions; and there's plenty of fish, suckers and trout, in Pine Creek to keep them healthy. I may have missed a photo opportunity in the gorge, but a winter rose blossomed in my thoughts and meditations.

6

A figurative winter rose wouldn't be substantial if it wasn't for the actuality of literal roses to support it through the warmer seasons of the year. Allow me to explain...

I've never been good at remembering people's names, and it doesn't get easier with age, but I recall a humorous experience relating to "Rose," and it occurred while fishing on a Pine Creek tributary.

It was a hot, humid day on Slate Run. Thunderstorms were forecast, but I was determined to fish, come hell or high water. I was wondering if the angling had improved, if the wild trout population had recovered from a disappointing ebb experienced in recent years. The flow was high from heavy rainfall, but I started catching small fish, and even had a large brown trout slam the dry fly, turn once on the surface, and disappear. This was more like it, I thought. Despite the heat and high water, Slate Run's fishery seemed to be on the mend; its future looked *rosier*, so to speak.

I saw a man about my age, or older, walking the streambank under the pines. I stepped out to say hello. I didn't recognize the fellow, whose name was Ed, but he knew me from the Slate Run Sportsmen meetings, and we quickly got to talking on the ways of people and trout. Ed is a fly-fisher, but he had recently broken his back—a circumstance that had forced him to use a cane or a walker on his Slate Run rambles. He enjoys painting, he said, and often works from a photograph that he's taken at the water.

Just before getting back to my fishing, I told Ed it was good to speak with him, and added, "What's your last name, again?" Ed's heritage is thoroughly German, and even though I've had plenty of experience with complicated names from the old country, I couldn't recall his last name. I *still* can't remember it, dammit. With due apologies to my new acquaintance, I knew it wasn't as simple as "Schmidt," or as difficult as "Wurzweiler," my mother's maiden name.

Ed provided his full name for a second time, and then recalled a joke he had to tell, saying, "You're a senior citizen, like me, right? Well, listen to this...

"An old couple came home from a dinner date at the restaurant. The old man and woman exited their car; and a young neighbor, who had known about their outing, saw the couple and decided to ask how the evening went.

"The wife had gone into the house, but the neighbor stopped the old guy just before he got away. *How did it go?* asked the neighbor.

"The old man said it went fine, not bad at all. Then the young guy asked him what restaurant they had gone to.

"Oh... down the road a bit. Not far.

"So, what did you have? What was the food like?

"Oh... I don't know, remarked the old fella, with some apprehension and concern. *It was pretty good, I guess.*

"What's the name of the restaurant that you and the missus went to?

"Oh shit, thought the old man. Now he's got me... *Uh, the name has something to do with flowers,* he said... *A spring flower... What's it called... with lots of smell and color, but with thorns.*

"Rose? Asked the neighbor. *Is it Rose?*

"Oh. Yeah, that's it! exclaimed the elder. He then put his hand beside his mouth and yelled to the house...

"Hey Rose! What was the name of that restaurant we went to?"

Ed and I departed, laughing loudly.

Winter rose, or spring rose, it's all just a name.

Small Stream, Big River

1

It takes about three hours to drive from Wiscoy Creek, in western New York, to the West Branch Delaware, east of Binghamton, in the Catskills. I didn't drive the route directly, but connected the streams on two occasions, six days apart. My reason for establishing the link has to do with fly-fishing, naturally. I wanted to continue the enjoyment of summer fishing for trout, but the land was hot and dry, and many of the streams were unduly stressed. The Wiscoy and the West Branch Delaware were in better shape, with cooler water, so their wild trout could be sought, if the angler fished with care.

Although rain and stormy weather was about to settle on my region for a while, the drought remained; and the toll that it was taking on our waterways appeared to be significant. The flows were reduced; and trout, a fish that struggles to survive when water temperatures climb toward the 70s (when dissolved oxygen levels are decreased) were having a difficult time. The Wiscoy and West Branch, though, were two of the possible exceptions in my fly-fishing realm. Despite some similarities in these two trout streams, there's a world of difference between them, too.

The Wiscoy, flowing through a level agricultural district in New York, is sustained by numerous springs and tributaries nourished by precipitation. It's a small creek feeding into the Genesee River near Letchworth State Park, and it's arguably the finest trout stream in the western sector of the state. The West Branch Delaware, on the other hand, is a Catskill Mountains tail-water flowing southward from the high ground just above the Cannonsville Reservoir (a water source for New York City) to its junction with the East Fork at Hancock, New York. There the two branches join and form the main stem of the Delaware River rolling southward into Delaware Bay and the Atlantic. It's hard to imagine a more disparate brace of waterways, but the Wiscoy and the West Branch are important streams. The Wiscoy is an unassuming little trout stream, and the West Branch is a world-class fishery that has been described as "the eastern-most *western* river in the U.S."

The big river has it all, from brook trout dwelling above the reservoir to giant browns that dine on a smorgasbord of possibilities including heavy insect hatches and the alewives that flush out from the dam near Deposit, New York. The fish can be highly selective at times, and the angler should attempt to cast precisely, or be skunked. The water volume can be heavy on occasion, even though controlled by the reservoir's release, and it's cold, even in the heat of summer. When I fish the West Branch, I tend to enjoy the experience and do okay on most occasions, but frustration also has its day, and getting skunked does happen.

Recently, I fished for two hours in the wind and sun, and the Delaware trout were a no-show. Despite a modest hatch of mayflies (Sulphurs and Cahills), no rises could be seen. Algae floated on the 55-degree water and snagged each cast of a wet fly. Drift boats passed me but, oddly enough, I didn't hear a hoot or a holler, typical expressions of a hook-up.

To fish a small stream like the Wiscoy, for contrast, was to cast with greater confidence at home. The water registered 63 degrees and was alive with surface-feeding brown and brook trout, at least for a short duration. I could cast a dry Black Ant and watch the rise; I felt the intimacy of a stream that helps produce what the writer Ted Leeson called the "archetype of fly-fishing." Here was a link to the earliest days of the sport, to the possibility that fishing the Wiscoy, and similar streams, was related to casting on the Greek river Astraeus, known to the Roman author, Aelian, who wrote of fly-fishing as early as 200 A.D.

Sure, the fish in the smaller stream are correspondingly more modest in size when compared to the specimens of the river. Modest, but delightful nonetheless. And undervalued, also, in today's big push to fish the best water available and to haul in its trophies for display. I don't care if the small fish of the archetypal streams are sniffed at by the hook-and-bullet press. I'm always proud to catch and picture them briefly, followed by release. Sometimes my better photos will be posted on my nature blog where readers understand that we take even the small fish seriously.

But fishing is catching, too, and the West Branch Delaware is a blast to angle on. It's not always easy work, to say the least, but a fisherman can enjoy great action there. Just recently, the night before my latest river stop, my friend Tim Didas caught a couple of massive browns while fishing the West Branch after midnight with ungainly streamers.

Then, of course, there's "culture" to consider when fishing the West Branch Delaware. The water isn't far from "Trout Town, U.S.A." (Roscoe) and Livingston Manor, home of the Catskill Fly Fishing Center & Museum where my wife and I make an annual visit to its Anglers' Summerfest. The history and magical presence of those Catskill locations are a doorway to a great beyond that I am still exploring. When the area's famous Beaverkill and Willowemoc Creek have warmed too much to fish conscientiously, there's always the neighboring tail-waters beckoning the compulsive flinger of a trout fly. The East Branch and the West Branch Delaware will absorb the fishing pressure handily. Even the distant Wiscoy can be thankful for that.

2

Wiscoy Creek is one of my favorite New York trout streams even though it's located well north of my preferred hill country. There's a lot of public water to be fished on this 20-mile stream before it enters the Genesee River, and I used to fish it regularly but, somehow, I got distracted.

It was good to get there on a recent morning. I had known about the wind turbines set up near the stream at Bliss, New York, but they weren't in operation when I visited a few years earlier. The turbines might be adding to the happiness of some Bliss landowners, but those monumental structures don't do a damned thing for the bliss of an arriving angler such as myself.

I felt apologetic for my lack of attention here. I'm a ridge-runner, I suppose, a curmudgeon, maybe, who prefers to fish the mountainous terrain of northern Pennsylvania rather than the flatlands of western New York—not that the Wiscoy is a slow-moving stream of level country, by ay means. In fact, the name *Wiscoy* is derived from an Indian term that means "five waterfalls," a reference to the stream's descent to the Genesee River valley. Nonetheless, the Wiscoy topography, compared to the rugged hill country of home, is relatively tame and uniform.

The Wiscoy is a wild gem flowing through agricultural lands. The Department of Environmental Conservation has established four or five parking lots for anglers along the stream, and footpaths to remote sections are often indicated by signs posted at the road. Perhaps the finest feature of this water is the trout—no stocked trout really, just wild fish, numerous brown trout and some brook that stay on the smaller side of beauty.

So, the ridge-runner parked his car, glanced at the windmills and the roadside ragweed blossoms (ugh!), and assembled his gear—an old 7-foot Phillipson cane rod and an even older Hardy reel (Uniqua) loaded with a 4-weight line, a tapered leader, and a number 20 Trico spinner. Perfect for the tight aquatic alley leading through the tunnels at the stream.

To be a ridge-runner I needed an element of authenticity. No, I couldn't just wander off to Hank and

Hettie Mae's to ask them for a quart of 'shine to be shared with whomever I met along the Wiscoy practicing good fly-fishing habits. Rather, I thought of the late James Glimm and his book *Flatlanders and Ridgerunners*, a collection of folktales from the mountains of Pennsylvania closer to home. I thought of two short tales the author collected that concerned the legendary Pine Creek browns...

Two friends walked along Pine Creek and one guy said to the other, "Yesterday I caught a trout that measured three feet long." His friend replied, "Yeah, well, yesterday I saw a lantern at the bottom of that pool right here, and it was lit." The first guy asked him, "You expect me to believe that shit?" His friend hesitated, then continued: "I'll tell you what; I'll blow out that lantern if you'll take a couple of feet off your trout."

The second tale concerns a Pine Creek fisherman who sat on the bank observing two large brown trout swimming around and biting each other in the nether regions until they separated to opposite ends of the pool. Each of the big 20-inchers turned and faced each other. Their mouths opened wide, and they charged ferociously. The fisherman looked on in disbelief. The trout had swallowed each other and completely disappeared!

The Glimm book, published by the University of Pittsburgh Press in 1983, remains a staple of my library and a folklorist's gem.

The Wiscoy's catch-and-release section near the headwaters at Bliss has always struck me as unusual for a special regulations water. This recovering farmland with its narrow stream of pools and riffles has a jungle-like appearance in the lush days of summer. Wading it for trout can be a challenge. I stumbled through the alders, paused at each new pool and watched for rises, then noted a transition in the feeding pattern when Tricos faded and Black Ants became the morning entrée.

A glistening brook trout and a smattering of browns came to hand before the rising heat of day began to quiet the water. Autumn was making its slow approach, and with it, the fishing would improve. For now, this archetypal trout stream, this retreat for ridge-runner and flatlander alike, was a fine place for a summer visit.

3

Heavy June rain at mid-week had raised the level of streams and rivers in the Catskill region to unfishable conditions. Things didn't look good for my weekend visit to the West Branch Delaware, but hope springs eternal, and I crossed my fingers to the possibility that the tail-water might at least be clear enough to roll-cast off the banks.

The West Branch, surely one of the finest wild brown trout fisheries in the eastern U.S., is a big river by most angling standards, with an average flow of 600-800 cubic feet per second (cfs). On my arrival at the Dream Catcher Estates on Friday, the river was pushing 3000 cfs and would remain at that force through my weekend at the fishing lodge.

I didn't catch any trout during my visit and neither did anyone else that weekend, with one exception. The small group of Trout Unlimited fellows in my company stood around watching large fish chasing alewives that had swept over the dam and swum downriver. We could take one step from the Estates' bank and suddenly find ourselves waist-deep in the powerful flow. We could make long sweeping casts of a white streamer with our nine or 10-foot rods, but those 16 to 21-inch browns were usually well beyond our reach.

The TU guys who had been at the lodge earlier in the week, before the river had drastically risen, had been luckier. They could wade across the river, and several of them had taken large browns on Sulphur flies or other small patterns imitating the various insects hatching from this well-known bug factory. But everything changed later in the week. At first, we tried for hook-ups by casting nymphs and emerger patterns. It *looked* as though the trout were taking just below the surface, then the truth came out.

George Hrycun and I decided to check on a small channel or braid that helped form a large island in the river. The channel was narrow and deep, and almost wade-able. Several of us would fall, either in the channel or someplace like it, going under to our chins. Luckily nobody lost his hat. But George saw a feeding trout and went after it with a streamer.

It had taken us a while to realize that the trout were chasing alewives swept down from the reservoir. The forage fish were everywhere and often sheltered in the flooded grasses along the channel. With the first cast of his streamer, George gave a shout. He had hooked one. Bring a camera!

The problem was I didn't have a camera. The memory disc of my waterproof instrument had become dysfunctional. I had just purchased a larger camera, a Nikon, and wasn't about to take it swimming with me. Then George remembered that he had a little camera in his vest somewhere. I floundered toward him through the water and the six-foot knotweed on the bank like a hippo gone berserk.

The wild fish measured 20 inches in the net. We quickly got a photograph and sent the brown back to the river. It was the only trout I got my hands on during this extended weekend on the Delaware. It didn't matter that I could purchase alewife imitations at the fly shop near our lodge. We couldn't get close enough to those big trout chasing small fish in the humbling river. Drift-boats would pass us; and the guides had clients casting streamers in every direction. Streamers would hit the water then get stripped in quickly before they sank. I'm sure some of those anglers had a great time fishing, not that I bothered to envy them.

Truth is, I enjoyed the visit. Hook-ups would have been a dream come true, but as a fisherman or two once declared, there's more to angling than simply catching fish. There were robins and thrushes that awakened me at dawn. There were bald eagles passing by the lodge, and an eagle's nest with young ones that I photographed from a distance. There were moments sitting at the kitchen table with friends while drinking Innis and Gunn. And there were excellent meals prepared by the Chef.

4

If fishing small streams like the Wiscoy is my modus operandi while angling through the day when visual links to the world around me are important, then night-fishing on a river like the Delaware is the dark side of the game—the difficult, the challenging, the thrilling aspect where the sense of vison is deliberately swept away for the chance to explore a realm of angling otherwise unknown.

If possible, I night-fish only with a trusted partner who knows the river as well as I do, if not better. Lately I have night-fished with a buddy, Tim Didas, an ex-Marine who really knows his New York waters. From a rainy night on Oatka Creek, where we pushed through foggy, shoulder-high shrubs and grasses to obtain a favorable pool, to the great starless wonder of the Delaware at midnight, we've done some crazy casting to the creatures of imagination.

To my way of thinking, life is too short for the serious angler to ignore the deep night. Admittedly, I'm not that serious about night-fishing to want to sample it more than a few times during the summer, but I don't feel complete as a fisherman if I don't give my own dark waters an occasional whirl.

During the summer the lunker browns and rainbows feed primarily at night. The best time to find them is on moonless nights when the warmth and humidity are close to being uncomfortable. One night, as Tim and I stepped into the West Branch Delaware and began to wade toward desirable casting positions, the midnight fog spread eerily across the quietude and stole the last shining star and then the distant lamplight.

It was like the world encompassed in a grain of sand. It might have been like a dream of owls, too. I'm not a superstitious fellow, but I try to respect the forces of nature, whether it's an unknown river that I'm wading, a mountain ridge that I'm hiking with a storm coming on, or the world of owls that I'm approaching with the hope of learning something new. I go easily, with the understanding that to be on guard is probably a wise thing to do.

I was listening to my own legs stirring up water as the river pushed and pulled around me, to the lifting of fly line from the surface as the rod initiated yet another hopeful cast to who knows where. I could have been listening to barred owls echoing each other with repetitive hooting in the night, in some way recognizing that a part of every human has a link to wild nature whether he or she can fathom it or not. Who knows? *Hoo*!

It was like fishing in ghost water, magnified a hundred times. I may have thought of Bootleg Hollow Creek, the small stream flowing by my house, a former home for native brook trout. Who knows? I sometimes muse about the fish conspicuous by their absence from that three-mile stream.

When I moved into the house in the early 1980s, I heard stories from local folks about the brook trout fishing in the creek. The fishing ended just a few years prior to my moving in. I used to walk the stream to have a look at what was in it. I imagined trout and mink and springtime warblers as I strolled along in May. No trout would ever come to my attention. The land and water had been abused; human lives had been wasted and abused; abandonment had occurred; the stream became my ghost water struggling to regain a life forever gone.

The deep night of the Delaware was rich with life and death. To fish it with flies was stimulating and intriguing if you played it right. With some planning and familiarity of water, you can have the river to yourself and get the spooky and exhilarating sense that angling is a whole lot more than you believed it was. When the big browns emerge from their hiding places and go hunting out in front of you, the sounds you'll hear will be amplified above the norm. The riffle splash will sound as though it's coming from inside of you; the headlight of a passing car may seem accusatory; the crack of underbrush along the bank might change a rabbit into a murderer; the slap of a beaver tail can shake you silly, but beyond all that the deep night will enfold you in the cradle of wild nature.

Yes, Murphy's Law, applied to the night-fisher, takes effect too readily. Safety should come first. It's good to have an angling partner who'll be there at the long end of a shout, if necessary, plus it's great to have the camaraderie and assistance when it's time to commiserate or to share your tales of glory. Tackle is important, too. I like to be prepared with an old 7-weight fiberglass rod, a short but flexible instrument equipped with a sturdy reel and floating line. If I trip and stumble off a bank, I much prefer to lose a cheap fly rod than to break a leg. As for artificial flies, I like to cast big bushy ones, the dark-colored wet flies, knotted to a stout leader tippet.

Whether fishing an archetypal stream like the Wiscoy in the light of day or casting on the Delaware with its wide range of insect life and water conditions, I enjoy the impact and immediacy of nature, and can only hope that everyone has a way to enter a similar realm, outside or in, and be renewed.

Spectacle Pond

1

Spectacle Pond lies in the heart of the Green Mountain State's Northeast Kingdom, a remote three-county area of Vermont where deep evergreen forests, glacial ponds and lakes cover the hills and valleys. Located near the modest and unassuming village of Island Pond (a former logging and railroading center now quietly accepting the tourist dollar), Spectacle Pond seems well-suited to representing the wildest and most remote section of this beautiful state.

In 2006 the National Geographic Society ranked the Northeast Kingdom as "the most desirable place to visit in the U.S." I'm not sure what criteria the venerable institution used to determine "most desirable places," so I won't argue the designation, satisfied to explore the place according to my own interests.

The pond is a small kettle lake (where ice entrapped in glacial debris has melted to form the current body) remaining largely undeveloped despite the presence of a state campground and a small campers' beach with boat rentals. A boreal forest with balsam firs, red spruce, and white birch surrounds the pond. The water is also noted for occasional moose visitations and for common loons that pierce summer nights with bird equivalents of cries and laughter.

I camped by the pond for several days and used it for my base to explore a bit of wild country east of Island Pond village. One plan was to walk the Nulhegan River Trail and fly-fish on a river I have never visited, but one that has held my fascination since reading of it in my trusty *Complete Book of Freshwater Fishing* when I was just a teen. The book, a very general but life-long guide, describes the Nulhegan as a river that "...drains Vermont's largest unpopulated area. Wonderful water."

I camped out at the pond after a night of tenting at Watkins Glen, New York where I had given a reading of poetry and prose and, later, listened to coyotes firing up the camp dogs with excitement. Next day, following a long drive to Spectacle Pond, it felt good to pitch the tent again and unwind. Blackberries fruited at the tent site, tempting an old naturalist to sweeten his caffeinated fare at breakfast time. The pond itself reminded me of what the Walden site may have looked like to Thoreau while the writer worked and meditated on its shore. I even heard a train roll by one night, perhaps a lost descendent of the nineteenth-century trains that passed by Walden Pond.

The moose population in the area is said to be the highest in the state, at more than one moose per square mile, but I wouldn't see the bog-and-forest dweller other than a bit of sign left at the water's edge. Other spirits of the place, however, were physically evident: an osprey hovered with an eye for perch and pickerel; a squadron of loons fished near the campsite and enlivened the nights with their sonorous, reverberant and haunting calls.

At camp, I could look across the water to Indian Point and be reminded of a quote about the place taken from an old railroad guide of 1853: "… Marks of Indian encampments and of their trails through the woods still remain; and a point which makes out into the pond… bears evidence of its use as the seat of council fires. The rounded point, clear of underbrush and smooth as a shaven lawn, is overshadowed by a growth of ancient pines, forming a complete shelter from the sun, while on either side and in front, the sheltered waters of this miniature lake are the picture of calmness and repose."

After taking several walks and fishing excursions along the wondrous Nulhegan River and then reading of Indian Point from the vantage of 1853, I was struck by what I thought might be an interesting idea. The pond's "rounded point" extends from the forest and is viewed as a sheltered place facing the placid waters of itself. A river can be rounded in imagination and become a wild pond or a lake, serene with poetry, flowing endlessly through the forests of the mind or just lying there before me in the actuality of loons and osprey. Lakes and rivers without end, one aqueous body whose source is the conception of a human soul and whose outflow is the ocean of death… A transcendental thought, for sure, but one that seemed to fit the time and place, even if the loons, so wild and free in our perception of them, might laugh hysterically from the peaceful wavelets out beyond.

2

It's good to have a secret pond. Ironically, once I talk about a secret pond it's not a secret anymore. Nonetheless, a secret pond exists; you'll have to trust me there.

The pond in mind is just an oblong waterhole originally designed for white-tail deer and its hunters. Located near my house, the pond looks deep and young. It's not a home for trout or even for bass—it has sunfish and a lot of frogs, and that's okay with me. If I arrive at the pond some clear summer evening, I imagine the several structures on my home place reflected from its surface.

When I fish the pond, I use a fly reel with a silent crank. There's no click to the turning handle. I hardly even know I'm fishing then. Frogs leap from the tall grass; bluegills shoot out from a resting place. I'm left there on the bank, alone. The pond is a blend of the pastoral and the wild. The field and forest are its neighbors; deer tracks are imprinted in the mud; I'm careful not to leave tracks of my own.

To have a secret pond is like having an erotic dream you'll never have to talk about. You might want to mention an exchange of looks and touches; you might want to tell someone close about the dream, but finding an adequate language is hardly worth the effort.

To acknowledge the presence of a secret pond is to say that your psyche (way down in the wildness of your head) is trying to tell you something. There's no point in calling Sigmund Freud or Carl Jung for assistance here. It's just a feeling you might get while standing at the pond.

To look at my secret pond on a summer evening is like waking from a dream remembering the words of Alfred E. Neuman of *Mad* magazine saying, "What, *me* worry?" I listen to the squawk of ravens; a chipmunk scampers through an old stone fence. I hear my breathing while I'm perched on a boulder near the pond, and my breathing says, "all clear."

The secret pond is both near and far, substantial as stone, ethereal as fog. A stream-walker like myself, a fisher of brooks and rivers, doesn't quite know what to make of it. He thinks of the pond as a stream that is basically round.

The pond is a source of poetry, too. The stream-walker doesn't write of it but makes a real connection with the pond. He doesn't talk about it much but, if pressed, he might tell you something new. Yeah, it's good to have a secret pond.

3

The Pond: Picking blackberries on my walk uphill, I came to the secret pond, a place for quietude and poetry. A short fly rod was assembled with a line, a leader, and an artificial fly. The lure I had tied was supposed to be an imitation of what could have been the first pattern in the western world constructed purposely for trout. This pattern was used by Greek fishermen in the days of the Roman Empire. I could make a delicate cast toward the reeds across the pond and pretend the fly was headed backward in time, across the ocean toward the reeds of Macedonia.

Here, surrounded by woods that look out toward the valley, I felt like a mongrel of a fisherman—partly pragmatic, partly poetic, and partly... nuts! Like anyone traveling off the beaten path. I felt excited, but for what? The possibility of catching a sunfish or maybe a bass? Like any mixed-up soul with an eye for science and a nose for nature's mystery.

I caught but a red-eared sunfish. No one else seemed to be around. My sunfish must have had a real adventure getting pulled out from the water, pulled into orbit like a visitor from an asteroid in Saint-Exupery's "The Little Prince." It lay there for a moment, cradled in my hand. The fish went back to the water with a splash, and with a word of warning for the other bream who lived close to the reeds.

The Lake: Normally, I fish the streams and rivers of my region, but recently I took a fly rod to the lake. This reservoir is unusual for the state—cold and deep, with trout and other kinds of fish. I don't like the fact that a dam has compromised a valley and its wonderful stream for trout, but the reservoir has aged, and trout can be caught from shore.

I could have used some practical advice on how to fish the lake, or perhaps prepared myself to *give* some practical advice to others planning a visit, but I fished as if the trout were close at hand, as if the lake's tranquility was a complement to productive angling. All I caught was a bass and several bream by casting a Woolly Bugger outward from the woods.

Preparing to leave, I put away the flies. Then a splash could be heard from the surface near the dam. A second splash got me digging for a popper with rubber legs. While sunfish slammed the popper, I imagined science and poetry mating there like dragonflies above the lake.

The Ocean: It all ends here eventually, the place where everything also begins. The ocean is the place where our breathing goes, the place that was here before our time, the place that stays long after we are gone. As the Seneca once declared, "Beyond all things is the ocean."

4

It seems that over the past few years I've made an annual, half-hearted attempt to catch a lake trout with an artificial fly, an achievement I have yet to accomplish. It's not that "lakers" are particularly difficult to catch with a fly rod, it's just that I am not a lake fisherman; I'm a stream and river guy, a fish out of water when I'm faced with miles of stuff that stays in place and doesn't seem to flow anywhere. And let's not talk about my lack of good timing for lake trout adventure, or the skill level that's required for hooking one of these North American chars.

It was a beautiful day in upstate New York, the first truly spring day of the year, with sunshine, stillness, and an air temperature rising into the 60s. A good day for lake trout fishing, maybe. Since I wanted new angling territory, I arrived at Canadice Lake, my favorite of the eleven Finger Lakes, a cold glacially-toned water that, for some reason, I had never fished before.

I was marking new ground, perhaps—leaving boot tracks on the wild eastern shore, learning something fresh about this place, putting something of my essence at the lake, an action not unlike a cat or a dog lifting a tail or leg, that says, "I was here; I'm probably harmless but I'm letting you know, anyway." I was looking at the lovely Canadice and facing the spectacle of Time, of Chronos, the great creator and devourer. Time had a way of speaking, as if to say, enjoy the season fully, my friend; this lake is wild as a bear and it's alive—like anyone who dwells here for a while.

Canadice is the smallest of the Finger Lakes, a 649-acre body with a shoreline of seven miles and a maximum depth of 83 feet. It's the highest Finger Lake, and the wildest and most remote, despite being only 35 miles south of urban Rochester. Along with neighboring Hemlock Lake, Canadice serves the water needs of the city, thus is sheltered from development while being surrounded by state forest lands.

Ice still covered the shallow north end of the lake. Standing in water near a launch site for canoes, I felt cold water pressing tightly at my waders. It was quiet here—no camps at the lake, no boats, no human voices other than a pair of hikers on the west side of Canadice, a half mile away. A gull shrieked, and a pileated woodpecker chortled from the pine-studded forest on the hills, but that was it for sound. If I hadn't known otherwise, I could have been casting on a pristine Adirondack water. And, as one might expect when an angler details the environment, the catching of fish was slow to non-existent.

No brown trout, rainbow or vaunted lake trout came up for the streamers I presented on a stout leader and sinking line. The water was still too cold, perhaps, too peaceful for success. The wild lake trout had yet to

153

approach the shores of Canadice. I could mark my territory at the lake and say that I'd be back some day, perhaps with a float tube or a different kind of naval device to augment my desire for deep-water trout.

To float with a tube or naval device doesn't guarantee success, of course. I remember messing about in a small boat that belonged to my friend, Tim Didas. We had arrived at Keuka Lake before the first light of a cold November morning. I fumbled with my gear in the darkness and prepared to fit myself into a life-preserver and a pair of oversized fins designed for attachment to my wading shoes. I took high, backward steps into the one-man pontoon, feeling like a fat bear entering a beehive in reverse.

I'm not a lake fisherman and have limited experience with fishing from a boat of any kind but was thankful for the loan of a pontoon. The small craft looked safer than the float-tube that Tim was navigating, at least from my perspective, on a big autumnal Finger Lake. Sure, a guy my age has had *some* experience with boats—at age five I'd taken a trans-Atlantic voyage with my mother on the largest ocean-liner of the time, and much later I'd gone drifting on a tin can in the middle of the Aegean Sea in a windstorm. And I've steered around in leaky canoes, but I was never in a situation quite like this before.

Keuka Lake has 58.4 miles of shoreline nestled in the grape-producing hills of central New York. Its cold, clear waters have a mean depth of 101 feet. Its fishery is almost legendary, once giving up a state-record brown trout weighing 23 pounds. Having lived near Keuka Lake for many years, I should know it better than I do, but I'm a stream angler unacquainted with fishing vessels. That said, I am slowly learning that a non-motorized craft can be a pleasurable tool and resource.

The little pontoon boat under my command was easily piggy-backed on a small car for transportation purposes. It proved to be so relaxing on the water (like drifting in an old recliner when I didn't have to paddle) that I fantasized about obtaining one for wild Canadice and Hemlock lakes. For now, the little craft would do quite well, indeed.

It took me a while to get the hang of casting from an easy chair, then paddling to keep ahead of the rising chop created by a strengthening breeze. We were casting streamers with the use of powerful rods. We drifted and paddled eastward from the lake's southern tip to the calm waters off Keuka Lake Inlet. The dawn's first effusions of light rose from the eastern hills and brought the ever-changing moments of new vision.

Tim caught the first and only fish on this excursion—a pickerel that initially seemed to be a landlocked salmon. A pair of tundra swans flew by us toward the marshes of Cold Brook and settled with a small flotilla of coots. I thought of Kenneth Grahame's masterful creation, *The Wind in the Willows*, and would later re-read the book's enchanting episode, "The Piper at the Gates of Dawn":

... Then a change began slowly to declare itself. The horizon became clearer, field and tree came into sight, and somehow with a different look; the mystery began to drop away from them. A bird piped suddenly and was still; and a light breeze sprang up and set the reeds and bulrushes rustling... Mole and Rat were

about to meet the piper demi-god (Pan) while on their quest to find a missing young otter.

I could look back to the morning lake and see the changes emanating from the eastern hills and cottages of Keuka with their glowing lamps. As if from within those glowing lamps, I had a vision of a spring day on the jewel of Canadice. Looking farther from this autumn view, while reaching backward to a summer day in the Northeast Kingdom, I could see reflections of the loons' pond off the shelter known as Indian Point.

Spring Seeps & Autumn Pools

1

After a long day's journey into and out of potholes, corrugated mud and rock, we finally settled to the sound of river music at night. We had driven 13 hours into northern Maine, left a frontier village for yet another hour's drive over gut-wrenching, white-knuckled roadway used by lumber trucks and recreational vehicles, then embraced the job of setting up our tent beside the dark, brawling river.

Next morning, I noted that we had passed the night just 20 feet from the West Branch Penobscot, with no one else around as far as I could see. I had probably never slept a sounder sleep. Our camp was near the gateway to the Allagash Wilderness and near the shadow of Mt. Katahdin. I had been here on a previous occasion, with wife and kids, but this time my wife and I were digging in. We would also visit Baxter State Park and Acadia National Park, followed by another camp-out in northwestern Maine, at Rangeley.

Good fishing was just a cast away from our grill site built from natural granite and river stones. It was good "fly-fishing only" water (the official designation), at least potentially. Wild brook trout and landlocked salmon swam among the deep currents and backwater eddies pouring from a dam two miles upriver. Fishing was slow because of late-summer conditions but fast enough to keep things interesting. I considered it a treat to find wild trout and salmon taking everything from a streamer to a dry fly.

A morning mist rose from a section of white-water called the Cribworks. Downstream, past the rapids, was a world-class fishing hole known as Big Eddy. Bald eagles, ravens, osprey, and various gulls flew between these river sites or perched with hungry anticipation on a large white pine or balsam fir. I fished an eddy near the tent and caught several small brook trout and salmon there. Rafters floated through the white-water, and I found it amusing to observe some occupants thrown out into the drink then rescued after a lot of shouting and swimming toward the boats. Their passage by the campsite was swift and hardly intrusive.

One night when the moon had risen, reflecting wonderfully from the small waves of the river, I entertained myself with night-fishing, knowing that the moonlight wouldn't help me catch much more than a dose of enchantment. Fishing would be better after daybreak and a meal of scrambled eggs, hot biscuits and coffee.

A fine landlocked salmon hit a Black Ghost streamer that I stripped in near our camp. The rod bent deeply, and I called out to my wife to come and watch the antics. These salmon are incredibly powerful, and even the little ones, when hooked, will sometimes leap high from the water. This larger salmon fought me hard and stayed on the line long enough to let its silvery flash and golden tones imprint themselves on the memory bank.

The name *Penobscot* has been translated from Native American to mean "place of descending rocks." It rained on our final day at the "rocks," pouring through my evening work-out with the rod and reel. I was switching my terminal tackle so relentlessly in the rain that I made a fool of myself, committing a wilderness faux pas that a loon could laugh about for hours…

I'd been casting into the driving rain for at least 10 minutes making graceful shots with the old "Maine Special" bamboo rod, before deciding to check on how the latest fly was doing… Uh, *what* fly? No wet fly, no streamer on, no *nuthin'*! Nothing more than the beauty of this stupid act, the madness of a so-called angler casting into the wind and water at dusk when no trout or salmon in the history of the art had yet to bite on a tapered line that has no hook.

2

The Kennebago River has been described as the third-best river in the continental U.S. for wild brook trout, after its neighboring flows, the Rapid River and Magalloway. The Kennebago was flowing low and clear on our visit in late August, but its well-known Steep Bank Pool was deep and challenging for the fly caster.

From a distance the pool looked more suited for carp and sunfish than for brook trout or landlocked salmon. I imagined that the quiet bend pool was a place where the river slowed from its descending pitch toward the ocean into a rounded formation like a warm-water pond before rocking onward in its typical course. But a rise from a trout would dispel that illusion; the water's depth and the steep forested banks would present a serious casting challenge.

Back in Rangeley at the fly shop, the proprietor was busy tying flies but took the time to help me determine the best way to fish the river. Her suggestions for fly patterns were also interesting. A local favorite is the old traditional Hornberg, a dry fly pattern I had known about but never cast—and the Hornberg did the job for me at the Steep Bank Pool. I caught and released a brook trout and a small salmon there but couldn't quite reach the larger fish rising beyond the limit of my casts.

The next day, on the deep riffles of Magalloway, I told an angler I had been the sole fisherman at the Steep Bank Pool, and he was surprised, saying that the pool is typically "shoulder-to-shoulder" at this time of year and that my wife and I were lucky to find it vacated. The Magalloway fisher was one of numerous individuals in the Rangeley district who helped us make connections in a friendly and informative way.

The owner of the Rangeley fly shop was familiar with a newly published book entitled *50 Best Places, Fly Fishing the Northeast*. I had written the book's chapter on Slate Run, and her husband, Brett Damm, a Master Maine Guide, had authored the chapter on the Kennebago River. I had learned that the name *Kennebago*, derived from a native language, translates into "people of the land of sweet-flowing waters." I think my wife and I met the multi-faceted spirit of the region as we camped near Rangeley and explored the neighboring streams.

The Cascade Stream Gorge Trail is a short hike near Rangeley Lake and is worth the time it takes to investigate its pools and waterfalls. Another beautiful creek (that I shouldn't name) is a primary spawning stream for brook trout in the area and a tannic wonder benefitting from restoration work by various groups including Trout Unlimited. I fished it one day with a barbless Stimulator dry fly, and the trout kept me busy hopping on the rocks until I tired of the action and my legs gave out.

The loons, screech owls and coyotes of Rangeley Lake provided all the midnight music that a camper could ask for. Speaking of the lake, I should mention that the second largest brook trout ever taken in Maine; a 12-pounder, was caught at Rangeley in 1890, spurring a fishing frenzy among Bostonians and New Yorkers. The *largest* brook trout ever caught in Maine tipped the scales at 14 pounds and came from nearby Mooselookmeguntic Lake (a name that only poets, madmen and moose could love). There was something like a gold rush to the Rangeley district at the turn of the twentieth-century. That gold had fins, and it swam among the sweet-flowing waters.

One of the most famous names in American fly-fishing is that of Carrie Stevens (1882-1970), who lived and worked near Rangeley. Her beautifully designed streamers, patterns such as the Grey Ghost and Colonel Bates, gained her international acclaim and are still considered to be among the finest ever tied.

We found the ghost of Carrie Stevens at the Rangeley Outdoor Sporting Heritage Museum in

Oquossic, Maine. This interactive museum also allowed us to study other local luminaries, people like Herb Welch and Fly Rod Crosby, as well as to speak with several bamboo fly-rod makers.

Out on the Magalloway River we met the Maine angler, Tim Arey, who had recognized the Slate Run Sportsmen cap that I was wearing. Arey was familiar with my home ground and had family who owned a camp near Sinnemahoning Creek in Pennsylvania. He and I became famous for 15 minutes on the hallowed Magalloway when we simultaneously fought our first landlocked salmon of the day. Mine had risen to a #8 Hornberg dry fly, of all things.

Earlier, my wife and I had eaten our lunches in a tavern across the street from the Outdoor Heritage Museum. I decided there and then that we were hovering in a timeless zone between the wonders of history and the hopes of days to come. I was fishing somewhere on the rounded, ox-bowed river of my time on Earth, between the spring seeps and the autumn pools of the flow, and for now the Maine woods swept outward from each new bank.

3

There was so much rain the week I spent on the upper Connecticut River that even my photos of the time got washed away. Not really, but the truth is that my wife and kids dropped me off, that rainy summer long ago, at Lake Francis State Park near New Hampshire's border with Quebec. They allowed me to deal with that incurable affliction known as "trout madness," to undergo a fisherman's trial by fire or, more accurately, a trial by inundation. They helped me to pitch my tents in a deluge of rain then left me to fend for myself with just my two feet for getting anywhere. The first rain event was a trigger to a week of monsoon weather while my family members enjoyed a sunny tour of Montreal and Quebec province. They absconded with my only decent camera and left me with the nagging certainty that I had no one to blame for my helplessness other than myself.

In addition to my fly rods and a week's supply of dehydrated food and drink, I had one disposable camera to photograph the vertical and horizontal flows of water. During my first night in the tent, the rain fell steadily till about 4 a.m. when the birds began to chirp relief and when a common loon began to shriek from the cooling waters of Lake Francis. Later, when the sun appeared for an hour or two, I made an admirable but futile effort to dry my clothes and camp equipment, the first of numerable failed attempts in the days to come.

The Connecticut rivertop is a tannin-colored stream flowing southward out of Canada through a series of dams and lakes. The Connecticut, all told, is the largest river draining the Northeast, and its upper section is a premium trout stream. I was camped out on the flow between First Lake and Lake Francis, a location convenient for an angler intent on catching trout or wild salmon, especially in favorable weather.

There were moose tracks in the river mud, boulders in the stream, and a flow of white-water that could probably match the volume of the run-off near my camp, but despite all the rain that first week in July, the upper Connecticut remained fishable because of the controlled release of water from First Lake Dam.

Although the river's appearance is that of freestone water flowing through a dense forest, it's a big stream that's released from the bottom of a lake, a tail-water that ensures cool temperatures for trout throughout the summer.

The Connecticut, averaging about 50 feet wide for the half mile that I fished each day, has a steep gradient. Water slammed against the mid-stream boulders forming rapids and deep eddies. A path through the boreal woods was marked "Fly Fishing Only." Here the river had to rank among the most attractive fishing locales that I've had the pleasure to find in the eastern U.S.

Unfortunately, the fishing wasn't as good as I had hoped for. Part of that assessment is due to all the rain, but I was a rookie here. I caught brooks, browns, rainbows, and even a few landlocked salmon that fell for my streamers and dry flies; but those catches were stretched over a week's worth of angling like a thin man fading into rain.

With a cup of coffee and binoculars in hand, it was fun to watch the loons paddling on the rain-spattered lake then swimming underwater for untold distances. The white-throated sparrows seemed to do their best to cheer my sodden bones by whistling five-note songs from lakeside shrubbery. At the Visitors' Center I asked about the weather forecast and was told, "Nothing different—just rain, heavy at times, today, tomorrow, forever."

I turned back to the river where the showers meshed with the darkened surface of the water. Wrapped like a green mummy as a shield against the rain, I would cast and watch the drifting line indicator. I caught a 15-inch brown trout on the last of my Grey Ghost streamers. When the Ghost was snagged and stolen by a deadhead in the roiling flow, that was it. I left the river to the winter wrens and Swainson's thrushes shuttling back and forth across the water feeding their young.

I was rescued by the tourists returning from "sunny Montreal." Their experience was a good one, certainly drier than my own. Would I recommend fishing the upper Connecticut to others willing to cast a line? Sure, but not in monsoon or hurricane weather. Although I sometimes felt like a loon surfacing from a deep swim in the lake, I enjoyed most of the adventure. On our homeward drive, the sun broke through the clouds; the river valley had become a shallow lake.

4

The Clyde River in the Northeast Kingdom of Vermont is listed as one of Trout Unlimited's "Top 100 Trout Streams in America" but it wasn't shining on my recent visit to the North Country. The river's headwater region looked too sluggish, boggy and warm for trout. The Clyde's major tributary, the Pherrins River, reputed to be excellent for brook trout, looked tired in this hot, dry weather and difficult to access. The North Branch Nulhegan, however, was a different story.

I found access at the mile-long Nulhegan River Trail off Route 105 near the Visitor Center of the Silvio Conte National Wildlife Refuge. Here was that trout stream I'd been dreaming of, one of three upper branches that had excellent water quality and, in cooler months of the year, good fishing for wild brook trout.

The upper Nulhegan drains about 150,000 acres of boreal forest and is also home to creatures such as moose, snowshoe hare, lynx, and spruce grouse.

On my first investigation of the North Branch, the river looked like a smaller version of the West Branch Ausable River in the Adirondacks. The river's guided trail was informative and enjoyable, and I knew that I'd be coming back later in the day equipped for fly-fishing. Eventually I would also hike a portion of the four-mile loop known as the North Branch Trail, another fine place to view the sub-boreal ecosystem.

Here the Nulhegan had a heavy flow of 65-degree tannic water averaging 30 to 60 feet in width. Its bed of glacial rock and boulder was a wading nightmare, but its pocket water was a restless beauty pushing hard for the distant Connecticut River, even in the sultry days of late August. I could have used a wading staff here but, minimally equipped, found that careful rock-hopping with studded shoes and shorts worked adequately.

The fishing wasn't much to write about, but I enjoyed it despite the difficulties. I made use of nymphs and streamers but didn't get a hook-up till I fished an Olive Caddis dry fly. The caddis pattern saved my work-out, luring two nice brook trout dark as a fir and about as eager to be photographed. Each of the fish leapt home before my camera got unzipped.

Later the next day I was homeward bound, myself, when I stopped in Manchester, that trendy town along the Battenkill River. After visiting the Orvis headquarters and the lovely American Fly-Fishing Museum, I settled into another night of camping, this time on the banks of the river once described as the location of "America's fly-fishing soul."

The Battenkill had just received an overnight flushing of rain that raised its level to twice the usual summer volume. I was ready for a skunking on what the writer John Atherton called in *The Fly and the Fish*, "the most difficult of rivers and yet the most rewarding in the things which count." A lot of skilled fly anglers have lived on or near this Green Mountain river because of the Orvis Company and the stream's long-standing reputation, and these mostly catch-and-release fishermen have shown the wild trout nearly every artificial on the continent.

The Battenkill is also a challenge by virtue of its physical character. The stream has a low gradient with long, slow pools interspersed with shallow riffles. The trout tend to hang along the banks where their food and shelter are secured. They can hold there with ease and carefully inspect each offering the smooth conflicting currents bring their way.

Concurring with the view of John Atherton, the angling writer John Merwin once described the Battenkill as "among the most—if not *the* most—technically difficult fly-fishing streams in America." Merwin rates it tougher to fish successfully than the Henry's Fork, the Firehole, the Letort (yes!), and Silver Creek, and he has had many years of wide fly-fishing experience. Okay then, I was humbled by the Battenkill before I even had a chance to venture into its rain-swollen water.

I had once fished the New York side of the Battenkill, but this would be my first entry into the higher Vermont stretches. The only other angler I would meet there claimed to be a Catskill rivers' guide with 30-years' experience who offered free advice on where and what to fish with. He would tell me that my nymphing rig might be okay if I knew how to work it properly in the deep water near the bank but, as for him, a devoted dry fly veteran, he was sticking to the surface.

It was good to out-fish the Catskill guide through our evening on the river. As he spoke to me about catching a 25-inch brown trout in our pool during the springtime hatches, I wasn't about to photograph the little 10-inch browns that I was catching on a Prince nymph while the others, big and small, ignored his Battenkill dries. The tugs of satisfaction that I felt throughout the evening kept on coming through the night. I slept with them, and with the sound of the river washing gently through my dreams.

5

The Parmachene Belle, a wet fly pattern named for Parmachenee Lake in Maine, was first tied by Henry Wells in 1878. Ray Bergman, author of *Trout*, brought fame to this pattern that had been tied, originally, for the brook trout of Maine's big lakes and headwaters.

Nick Karas, in his book called *Brook Trout*, repeats the story of a legendary trout caught from the Nipigon River in the late nineteenth-century. The subject of this narrative is a 14.5- pound brook trout that was hooked and landed with a Parmachene Belle, the wet fly that was then a local favorite.

According to Bergman, in *Trout*, the Belle is a popular fly that substitutes an imitation of the paired fins of a brook trout for the usual imitation of a natural insect. The original pattern by Henry Wells opened the field of wet fly patterns to allow development of the modern streamer fly. Bergman claims to have fished it successfully in high and discolored water. The beautiful proportions and pleasantly contrasting colors of the Parmachene Belle have kept the pattern alive and well past its 100th birthday, and they're likely to keep it vibrant for decades to come. The recipe:

Hook: TMC 3761; 10-16.
Thread: Black 6/0.
Tail: Red and white hackle fibers, mixed.
Rib: Fine gold flat tinsel.
Body: Yellow floss.
Hackle: Red hen and white hen, mixed.
Wing: Married sections of red and white duck quill segments.

The married quill wings are the essence of tradition reaching back to the salmon and sea-trout roots of the British Isles, and the probable reason that I have yet to tie the Parmachene myself (wingless wets are friendlier to my elementary tying skills).

When my sister, Barbara Lyng, a stained-glass artist, agreed to build a custom fly for me in glass, it didn't take me long to decide which pattern to propose. The result of her project with the Parmachene Belle is a beauty that now hangs against an eastern window of my house. It brings a touch of warm tradition in the cold days of winter, and my glance at the Parmachene in Glass renews my angling spirit as it drifts along in memory from the spring seeps to the autumn pools of the year.

When I asked my sister via email how the Parmachene project came to be and how it developed, she replied in detail. The process sounded vaguely familiar and pertinent. For that reason and more, I include Barbara's full report:

My favorite parts of the process are picking out the proper glass, designing the project and enjoying the finished work.

When designing I must keep in mind that you can't just place a bird, for example, in the middle of the sky without lines going to it. Circles and curves are possible but have more glass waste than straight lines. I try to have as little waste as possible.

When selecting the glass, each piece is held up to a bright light to see what the end effect will be. Some glass looks fantastic but is blah when held up to the light. And vice versa. Then all the pieces chosen must be viewed together in the light to see how they complement each other. The actual site the finished project will hang in also affects what color is chosen.

After drawing the project on paper, it needs to be enlarged to actual size. Then the chosen glass pieces are laid out to see if the design needs to be modified. Most glass has a direction of pattern, so that must be considered.

A paper pattern is then cut out for each piece of glass. The pieces are then cut, ground, washed, foiled, washed again, soldered, and washed yet again. Then the frame is made; a patina is applied, the whole project is washed once more, and a chain is attached for hanging.

The process for designing and developing my Parmachene in Glass reminded me, somehow, of the book that I was writing. There was a connection in the step-by-step and in the outline of the finished products. Whereas I could work with the language of a student in the field and on the trout stream, Barbara was employed by glass and vision.

Parmachene Belle lies on the water.

Wings Over Water

Frankly, I don't make much of a living, but I make a hell of a life.

– Jack Gartside

1

There were plenty of quiet moments at the book signing event, so I was glad to have some fly-tying stuff at hand. My books were piled on a corner of a table in the store; my vise stood before me, surrounded by olive grizzly hackle, calf-tail, dubbing, moose hair, thread, scissors, whip-finisher, everything needed to tie the Western Green Drake for an upcoming trip out West. Everything was here, except the hooks. Dammit. Without the hooks, I felt like a wingless bird showing up late for spring migration.

Now what? The store managers were busy doing whatever managers do when business is slow. I rose from my seat and began perusing the Used Books section of the aisles, deciding then to buy a hardcover edition of the *Tao Te Ching* in order to refresh my understanding of the ancient Chinese classic. Chapter One: *The Tao that can be told is not the eternal Tao.* Of course. Words get in the way. *The name that can be named is not the eternal name...* The fly tier who forgets his hooks is not worth his hackle. He becomes just another purchaser. The gate to mystery has a squeaky hinge.

The highest good is like water. We moderns who enjoy canoeing, hiking, fishing, etcetera are aware of this. *Water gives life to the ten thousand things and does not strive. It flows in places men reject and so is like the Tao.* Water filled my head like dreams... I would soon be fishing on the Oz (my name for Oswayo Creek).

The Oz, or Oswayo Creek, was flowing heavily from a recent storm. The sky was overcast; the prospect for a hatch looked pretty good. Two spin-fishermen were working downstream toward me while I stood in a deep, expansive pool. One guy asked if I was fishing the Derby or just fishing. Since I didn't know anything about a local Rod 'n' Gun Club Derby happening at the time, I simply answered, "I'm just fishin'. Any luck?"

I wasn't feeling particularly wise there in the company of two locals chasing tagged trout with the spirit of a horse-better at the Preakness. And I wasn't keeping my mouth shut, either, when the guys inquired as to where I started from and what pools had yielded trout. *The sage goes about doing nothing, teaching no-talking. The ten thousand things rise and fall without cease.* In my defense, I stretched the truth a bit describing the character of the pools I fished. They were tough, and the trout weren't rising to a dry fly. There were no ten-thousand trout rising and falling to a mayfly or a caddis hatch.

I was honest about the surface action. It was almost non-existent. I was hooking trout—hatchery

173

fish—on streamers, especially with a conehead Woolly Bugger. These were not ideal conditions on the Oz, but at least I was fishing.

Earlier in the day, before my scheduled book signing at the store, I had the best time watching birds. Spring migration was at its peak, and numerous fliers had settled near the yard for the season or were pausing for insects and tuning up their vocal chords. I, too, attempted to hone my skills with 10-power binoculars and a late-spring shuffle. Birds, as always, enlarged my neighborhood of thought and gave me a key to a realm beyond myself, a cosmos they belonged to that transcended the limits of any town. I agree with Thoreau, who said a wild bird is a true citizen of the land, reflecting a place in both its solidity and abstraction. I would add that wild trout are a similar spirit. Bird and trout—winged and free, or finned and free—take me to a glorious room without walls. A natural experience.

For now, beauty seemed to outshine ugliness. Barn swallows lilted over the roadway scarfing up midges near the ground. An indigo bunting fed among the apple blossoms, its plumage slightly darker than the sky beyond. A Tennessee warbler (not the same as a Nashville *crooner*) sang a loud migration song, its chip notes breaking into a jumble at the end. A wood thrush piped an endless three-note song; a Baltimore oriole perched nearby, the orange-and-black songbird whistling and fluting for a mate in a timeless quest for continuity and survival. Beauty was a victor, even as a raven chased a red-tailed hawk across the southern sky.

Under heaven, all can see beauty as beauty only because there is ugliness. All can know good as good only because there is evil. Listen to the news from around the globe today and go for the truth. I remember a comment by the late American poet, Charles Bukowski, who said, "The problem with the world today is that the intelligent people are full of doubts, while the stupid ones are full of confidence." With that in mind, I am thankful for the wild birds, for the wild trout, for the wildness in men and women, for the children who can tell what's real and what is fake.

2

In early June, I continued to keep an eye out for insect hatches on the local streams but wasn't seeing much yet. Oh, the Sulphur mayflies made an afternoon appearance on Cross Fork Creek. A few March Browns came off the Genesee River (less spectacular than the decent spinner fall at dusk). Some Green Drake and Coffin Flies appeared on Kettle Creek, the East Fork Sinnemahoning and Birch Run, but basically the hatches for this time of year seemed underwhelming, perhaps due to all the high water of late.

Whereas the fishing had been slow, compensation came from friends and songbirds taking up the slack. I had good conversations with anglers on Cross Fork Creek while watching sulfurs and swallow-tailed butterflies. Fishing buddies Tim and Don shared pleasant moments with me on the dusky Genesee as spinner flies sailed to the water to be intercepted by cedar waxwings and song sparrows, or to be sipped by rising trout. A veery chanted hauntingly and a hermit thrush caroled from a hemlock grove, their throats and wings a vibrancy of life above the water.

One morning I took a hike into the higher realms of Birch Run, a stream fraught with tight arboreal growth and irritating gnats. The venture proved the adage that "the higher you go, the better the fishing gets." All I needed was a short fly rod and a small dry Adams on the line. The brookies were accommodating and the raspy robin-like song of scarlet tanager lent a soothing aura to the shadowed greens of early June.

For a change of pace, I returned down-valley to the Sinnemahoning. The overcast sky remained a blessing; and the valley breezes blew away the pestering gnats. The creek seemed full of hatchery trout from 10 to 14-inches long, willing to chase a drifting Adams. Most welcome, too, were several brook trout adding wild color to a somber hour on the creek. Although the local streams were flowing high, the rising water temperatures seemed to spur the trout on a feeding frenzy near the surface. Hatch activity was minimal, so the classic Adams, the generic caddis/mayfly pattern, was all I needed for an artificial lure. Simplicity, when you find it, is a wondrous thing.

3

My opportunity to fish the Driftless area of western Wisconsin was more like a homecoming than a clear response to all the good angling press the region has received over the last few decades. I spent my high school years in La Crosse, Wisconsin but had to leave the area after graduation, before I could fully appreciate the outdoor benefits that came with living there.

We were traveling homeward from a trip out West. By the time we reached Minnesota on the eastward drive, we were tired but looking forward to the prospect of a restful fishing stop in Wisconsin's Driftless region.

Surprisingly, I can still remember some of my school years in Wisconsin. I hunted small game near Viroqua in 1967, and even trapped muskrats that year in the Mississippi River sloughs. I still have my stamped fishing license from '67 but don't recall ever casting a line for Driftless trout when I was young. Clearly, in 2018, it was time to make amends.

The last wave of glaciation never drifted into the southwestern part of what is now Wisconsin, so the soil is rich and loamy, a boon for dairy farming through the last two centuries. I don't think the brook and brown trout fishing was much to get excited about when I attended high school in the late 60s. If it was good, well, I was too preoccupied with other things to really care about it. But the angling took off later when environmental issues came to the fore, when landowners, state officials, and groups like Trout Unlimited started working for stream improvements and the benefits derived from recreational pursuits.

We left our Wildcat Mountain campsite early in the morning and visited Viroqua, Wisconsin and its Driftless Angler Fly Shop where the help that we received for my ensuing day was excellent. The folks at the shop had everything conceivable for the visiting angler, and their guidance for my first real look at the Driftless water was essential. We were soon on our way to Coon Valley and the charming *coulees* where fly-fishing with barbless hooks not only makes good sense for many, but also is required as part of the catch-and-release regulations established for various sections of the streams.

The weather on that July day was horrible—hot and humid, with the morning punctuated by thunderstorms that only seemed to irritate and madden the mosquitoes and blackflies while enhancing the sultry air and darkening sky. I had asked a local dairy farmer if I could fish his pastures, and he was fine with that, but I got turned around and frustrated with fencing obstacles that barred me from trout rising in the pools, so I hastened a retreat from the barnyard and its herd of inquisitive Holsteins.

My wife and I went for lunch in Coon Valley, and after that our situation improved. The weather remained hot, but the afternoon looked better for a friendly get-together with the trout. I found an attractive stretch of meadow stream (sometimes reminiscent of a spring creek in the East), with pools and riffles and a water temperature of 62 degrees. A stiff breeze seemed to banish all the biting insects, and the streamside cows acknowledged me as just another crazy fisherman. I was wet-wading, and all was sanguine with the world.

I quickly caught and released six wild browns on a small Black Ant. Several of the fish were not only colorful but easily a foot in length. A couple of larger browns were hooked and lost, as well, and I had a feeling that some hefty trout inhabited the stream. Chester the fly rod, my faithful bamboo, had a healthy work-out in the Driftless afternoon, and I'm glad I didn't need him to intimidate an angry bull.

It was time for us to head on home, with a brief stop for local wine and cheese, and even for a photo op with sandhill cranes. The long-necked birds were feeding in corn stubble, and my first good look at this species takes wing in my memory, even now. The cranes seem to fly in our transition from west to east, adding to the sense of gladness that we drifted into the Driftless after my years of absence. It's an understatement to say, certainly, that my visit was better than a class reunion.

4

I was sick of all the news saturated with senseless violence and political mayhem. I was feeling burned by the reality of drought and floods and frequently occurring "thousand-year weather events" across the globe. I could not get used to the fact that water levels on our regional trout streams had dropped precipitously while their temperatures had risen to levels dangerous for fish. I knew I had to get over it all, if only for a little while.

Our old kitchen was getting torn down for replacement. Maybe I could take a hint and have my "soul kitchen" updated, reinvented, so to speak, renewed with a visit to elsewhere. And where would that be—Maine, Montana, Michigan? No, not yet. I headed for the evening woods across the road from my front yard.

The forest climb and the meadow vistas were relaxing and serene. I could investigate the forest gloom and see the brightness of a soul at peace with itself, at peace with the chorusing of hermit thrush. I could gaze across the hilltops and perceive the place where I languished when the blues afflicted the mind and heart. I could see that solitude might be defined as the occasion when we are in the company of non-human nature. I could put my place of life in perspective by absorbing the sunset and the quiet entry of the stars above. I could do all these things but there was no escape for my unsettled thoughts.

What I had in mind for a series of evening walks was to do a natural inventory because the physical landscapes that surrounded me would soon be changing, thanks to mankind and the need for increased energy consumption. The wind turbines were coming and likely to be installed within two years.

I've got nothing against wind power, per se. We need to shift our use of dirty fossil fuels to cleaner, more sustainable energy alternatives. I've seen the giant turbines in numerous locations near and far and prefer their use over coal extraction, hydro-electric and nuclear energy (30 years ago I fought tooth-and-nail against a federal and state proposal to dump nuclear waste here at the rivertops, but that's another story).

On a good day when I'm feeling generous, I might even say that I like wind power, and acknowledge the possibility that I'm a wind generator, myself—another story better left unstated. But wind power generation has be installed correctly and with all the best environmental studies incorporated. Installation requires an increased sense of social and global responsibility. I don't trust our current guidelines for their placement on these lands, nor do I trust the handiwork of out-of-state energy corporations with their plan for us—a cold design that looks like an invasion of rural life and its relative stability.

I don't want to see turbines set up on the bat fields or on a major migratory route of songbirds and golden eagles, and I don't want to see them from my backyard. I'm a NIMBY when it comes to the installment of 600-foot windmill turbines, and I say not-in-my-back-yard. Why so?

A lot of people claim to like them in their neighborhood. They don't seem to mind the noise of turning blades or the constant flicker of light. The towers look metallic, brilliant, kind of futuristic in the "wind farm" format that's presented to the public by the energy corporations. Turbines make us look richer, they say, more middle class, aspiring toward the upper crust of society. And they're helping us save the Earth, aren't they? Well, not really.

Here, among the hills of home, the big turbines are already present in some locales, and more are coming. Currently there are 176 more of these behemoths (each one taller in its reach than the Washington Monument) proposed for a 15-mile swath of land including my home. High-voltage transmission lines will accompany the 600-foot structures, and the wind companies say don't worry—the people who live with turbines (and profit from their placement) have no complaints at all.

But some landowners/lease-holders sign an easement for installation that is tantamount to a gag order preventing them from voicing public complaint for up to 45 years. As for the effect of these installations, turbines will have little impact on decreasing carbon emissions, but they'll make a big impression on the natural environment and the health of rural life.

Unless we decrease our consumptive habits and diminish our growing use of—dare I say it—computers and electrical gadgetry, we're only increasing our ability to consume more and more of what is left to be consumed. The turbines are here, and they will mushroom till the corporations enter bankruptcy and leave their monuments behind. I won't wax Quixotic and go tilting at those giant blades (there are easier ways to get scalped), but I won't go down easily, either.

I'm a NIMBY on this issue because I moved here some 40 years ago to escape from similar industrial reminders. I moved here to find rural peace, to be near trout streams and hermit thrushes, as far from the madding crowd and the "ignoble strife" as I could afford to be. And so far, it's been good. We dodged the spectacle of a nuclear waste dump in Allegany County; we dodged the bullet from hydrofracking of Marcellus and Utica shales in New York State (but not in Pennsylvania). The turbines may not be so bad, comparatively speaking, but they'll change the land and skyscape irrevocably; they'll always recall the world of mass murder and political mayhem that's around the bend. They'll have yet another major impact on the hills and valleys; and no, the out-of-state industries won't be putting many residents to work, either.

So, I'm doing inventory for the head and heart. My camera is ready, too. I'm enjoying the summer woods and meadows, seeing them in ways that give me peace. To paraphrase a biblical sentiment, I could say that here the grey coyote dwells with the spotted fawn; here the black bear of the body lies down with the singing thrush of the soul. The kitchen of the spirit is renewed and refurbished, for now.

5

If you drive around Albemarle County, Virginia long enough, you'll eventually leave the rolling hill country of the uber-rich and find yourself in the humbler Appalachian vales near Stone Mountain. There, not far from Dyke, Virginia, the *real* fun of looking for Stone Mountain Vineyards begins.

The Blue Ridge Mountains, west of Stone Mountain, will advertise their beauty. You'll likely miss the dirt road turn-off to the winery a couple of times, but that's okay. Don't bother relying on a GPS unit because your monitor will read "Entering unknown area, use caution," or something similar. Your car's computer will be whacked by the presence of a road that jumps 1700 feet, from sea-level altitudes to the sky, in a matter of several hundred yards of lateral movement.

If you've ever dreamed of driving up a hill so steep that your vehicle flips over front to back, you won't enjoy this climb. But it's not so bad. Bolivia's "Death Road" is reputedly more dangerous. Sure, this Stone Mountain climb is not so much a roadway as it is a rutted goat path (I exaggerate), a dirt track with no guard rail or even a recognizable pull-off. And once the climb begins, rest assured there will be no turning back. You just lean forward, pray (if so inclined) that no one else is coming around that hair-pin curve above you, or just hope like hell that you will make it.

You arrive at the beautiful, rustic winery built into the side of the mountain. You enter and ask the tour guide, "How 'bout that road?" You'll get a nod that seems to say, "Nothin' to it; we're here even in winter, though we're closed December through February." That said, you've earned your drinks.

You can buy a modest tasting of 11 different wines, or a slightly more expensive tasting of 15 different wines. If you're as ignorant about wines as I am, you'll agree that the overall quality is better than average. The company I kept on this heavenward excursion seemed to favor the Cabernet Sauvignon and Chardonnay, buying a few bottles for the trip back down to Earth.

I rested on the wrap-around deck attached to the winery. I had to believe I had the finest views from any winery in the Old Dominion. I saw the distant piedmont region and the Southern Mountains. I was thankful that our vehicle had good brakes and tires to enable us to reach this air of vultures, hawks and eagles. Hopefully they'd be good for our descent, as well. I fixed on a thought about golden eagles—that to borrow an eagle's wings for flight above the skyline would be wonderful, indeed.

I've studied golden eagles since 1993 when I saw my first migratory golden in New York. I've seen this raptor (relatively rare in the East) every year since then, most often during the spring and fall migration, in both New York and Pennsylvania, as well as in the wilder sections of our western states. One autumn I saw a group of four or five migratory goldens over the Ridge Road near my house. Sightings such as this concern me, now that windmill turbines are proposed for the ridge and other landmark places utilized in migration.

I could gaze westward from my winery perch, as sober as an ornithologist on duty, and see as if I had flown on wings. Out there—in the distance of our land, the lower elevation of a *southwestern* desert, and the high terrain of arid mountains. Out there—the country of Apache and Gila trout, the wild fish surviving, barely hanging on, its suitable habitat long erased. We humans have exploited the wildlife and resources there for millennia. The region's water has been irrigated into nothingness. The land gets as brittle as gold-leaf; fires claim the higher trees and vegetation. Rainbow trout and other non-native species invade the cold streams that remain. The gene pool of cutthroat trout evaporates dramatically and yet the native fish survives in the high, remote mountains.

The late trout historian and biologist, Robert Behnke, has said (I'll paraphrase): Transition occurs as one moves from the desert valleys toward the mountain headwaters with their cooler climate and greater precipitation. Vegetation shifts from cactus and sage to mesquite, pinyon and juniper, oak and sycamore, then to aspen and the conifers. There the wet meadows (*cienegas*) act like giant sponges that retain the snow-melt and rain that slowly drains and feeds the headwater streams for trout.

My view from Stone Mountain glosses Behnke's work with native trout. I've visited the Southwest and explored it in numerous locations; I return there for several minutes with my golden eagle of a daydream, thinking… *how about that road….*

Here, the Blue Ridge Mountains deepen in evening light, the indigo shadows reaching eastward across the valley like somnolent waves on a shore. It's time to drive back down. In a well-built vehicle, perhaps in a car with wings… A vineyard visitor has another idea. He says, you'd be better off "in a piece-of-shit pickup truck that's borrowed from a friend."

6

March 1st: Inspired by the new month and slightly warmer temperatures, I decided to climb Dryden Hill through the falling snow and see if I could reach the old tower behind the house once owned by Pete McKenna. An abandoned steam thresher (ca. 1930s) might still be found there by the old tower in the woods. I had once written about another local, Dan Redmond, and his farming days of "custom threshing." Now I wanted to inspect the antiquated machinery.

It was an arduous 40-minute ascent along the old seasonal roadway to the former McKenna farm and then the summit of the hill, with no real track to ease my walk except for the paths made by numerous deer. I saw only an occasional chickadee, a passing crow or raven, and a couple of ruffed grouse startled from the pine trees. Other than the stronger light produced by the late season, there were no signs of approaching spring as far as I could tell.

The wind and snow were more intense along the summit, and I was able to advance but a short distance from McKenna's house toward the old tower site. The crusted snow was up to my knees with every step. Without snowshoes, I quit the effort and began my return. Did the tower and abandoned thresher remain there, inside the woods beyond the pond, or had they been dismantled and removed? Only an investigation in warmer weather could provide an answer.

March 14th: I had no fly-fishing this week-end but I tied a handful of "back in black" stoneflies and Woolly Buggers in anticipation of the settling of streams and, also, to feed or nourish the first few sprouts of imminent spring. After that I made another slow climb of Dryden Hill.

Although the wet snow of the woodlands was still deep enough in places to engulf me to the knee-caps, there were patches of summit fields where the snow had melted and was rushing downhill in a welter of chaotic rills. Small bands of migrating robins could be seen on the swaths of brown frozen earth, hungry for the first slimy tubes of life emerging in the new year. Reinforced by the taste of scarlet rose-hips pulled from thorny bushes in the desolate afternoon, I approached an old piece of machinery that I mistook initially for the steam-powered thresher once used by the likes of Greenwood farmer, Dan Redmond.

Years ago, when I last encountered Dan, I noted that the 84-year-old life-long resident of the area was square-jawed and very muscular for his age. We conversed amiably about his days as an agricultural thresher, as well as on other subjects he was passionate about. He had seen great changes through the century, and he spoke about their impact on the land and people. As he spoke, Dan noted that his hearing aids were "behaving"; he could hear my questions well, so he was comfortable chatting with someone who would listen.

I thought about Dan as I noted the mysterious machine in front of me, a long box of rust and wheels still dignified where it lay beside the woods, a warm patina from the decades wrapped around it like a coat. Had he been there physically, Dan would have corrected my assumption right away: "No, that's not a thresher. It's a grain separator. Follow me." So, I walked with Dan, in spirit, to a much larger machine at rest inside the trees, not far from the former site of a small communication tower.

I saw the profile of a great reptilian device. I was surprised that in all my years of hill climbing and wandering I had never really taken notice of it. Standing near the rusted but remarkably well-preserved threshing machine, I tried to imagine Redmond's renowned style of hand-feeding the bundles of wheat.

I had learned a few things about threshing from a pamphlet written by Harriet Redmond, Dan's wife, and published by the Greenwood Historical Society in 1990. Dan's father and uncle had worked a threshing machine, like the one I found here in the woods, powered by a horse-drawn steam engine and a water tank. Three teams of horses were required to haul an entire threshing rig from farm to farm, the job of "custom threshing."

Dan Redmond was 12-years-old, circa 1920, when he first started feeding grain into a thresher. He followed his father's footsteps till about 1945 when the threshing era was replaced by mechanization symbolized by the more efficient combine. In my conversation with him, several decades back, Dan reflected on the changes. All too many people had become disinterested in their land, beyond its monetary value. For example, many landowners interested in lumbering their properties had abandoned the use of horses in favor of destructive practices ensuring a quick and easy haul. Dan knew about the ecological value of trees and had become an ardent planter of various species later in his life. He planted on cut-over lands and on swampy acreage where he found that native pines grow well. He reminisced about the great American chestnut tree, how he, too, had collected chestnuts before the blight developed and demolished the last of the species in the Appalachian districts.

"Trees give us more than most of us suspect," he told me. "I planted trees to give something back to nature when agri-business took so much away." The breakdown had come. Community spirit was dissolving. In present time, I thought about the next phase of the changes as I saw them. I thought about the massive turbines, windmills, coming to these ridges and these hilltops. What could I give, as an antidote, of sorts, to what the modern age was taking from the land?

I tried to imagine it: *hand-feeding bundles of wheat to the machine, a grain of wheat being separated from the chaff inside—pulled and tossed by steel claws and rapidly moving arms, encountering a bar with teeth, hearing the rollers whir, feeling the quake and rapid descent into a slotted surface perforated with holes, getting shoved by a blast of air removing the chaff, and being lifted into a bucket, one more kernel added to the load...*

Ah, the purity of grain! A new season threshed out by the wheel of time. A cosmos risen out of chaos, seeds of springtime fleshed out like a bird in flight, or a trout that's nabbed a fly. The river of life in its entirety. And all that I could do was glimpse it and reflect on what I know—from source to confluence, summit to ocean, rill to valley bend, each root and rock, each bird and fish, exposed and then forgotten. It was one sensation, like a puff of steam—the ghost in the thresher, the machine.

About the Author

Walt Franklin is a writer, educator and environmental activist who ventures outdoors as much as possible. He is an active member of organizations such as Trout Unlimited and Slate Run Sportsmen. His published non-fiction books include *A Rivertop Journal*, *River's Edge*, *Sand & Sage*, *Beautiful Like a Mayfly*, and *Streamwalker's Journey*. His published poetry volumes include *The Wild Trout*, *Uplands Haunted by the Sea*, and *Earthstars, Chanterelles, Destroying Angels*. He and his wife, Leighanne, reside in rural Greenwood, New York.

Check out his regularly posted fly-fishing and nature blog at **www.rivertoprambles.wordpress.com**

www.ingramcontent.com/pod-product-compliance
Lightning Source LLC
Chambersburg PA
CBHW030011290326
41934CB00005B/301